From Darkness To The Wonderful Light

One Man's Journey in Poetry

Peter James Martinez

From Darkness To The Wonderful Light

First Edition

ISBN – 13 978-475236910

ISBN – 10 1475236913

Library of Congress Control Number: 2012938588

Published by JRWJK Publishing Company, LA
Editor: W. James Johnson, Ph.D.
Design and layout by W. James Johnson, Ph.D.

Pictures copyrighted by FreephotosBank.com

Printed in the United States of America.

JRWJK Publishing Company
5807 Old Boyce Road
Alexandria, LA 7130

Contents

Title	Page
About The Author	8
Foreword	13
Acknowledgments	14
Disclaimer	16
Introduction	18
Title #1: Beware Statement of Enlightenment 1	19 21
Title #2: Changing The World Statement of Enlightenment 2	22 24
Title #3: Free Yourself Statement of Enlightenment 3	25 27
Title #4: Giving Thanks Statement of Enlightenment 4	28 30
Title #5: Jesus Statement of Enlightenment 5	31 33
Title #6: Justified Statement of Enlightenment 6	35 37
Title #7: Lost Then Found Statement of Enlightenment 7	38 40
Title #8: Sad Truth Statement of Enlightenment 8	41 43
Title #9: Remembering Statement of Enlightenment 9	44 46

Title	Page
Title #10: Selfish	47
Statement of Enlightenment 10	49
Title #11: Shell of What Was	50
Statement of Enlightenment 11	52
Title #12: Who's Game	53
Statement of Enlightenment 12	55
Title #13: What I'll Say or Do	56
Statement of Enlightenment 13	59
Title #14: Keep Faith	61
Statement of Enlightenment 14	63
Title #15: Limitless	64
Statement of Enlightenment 15	66
Title #16: Hardening	67
Statement of Enlightenment 16	69
Title #17: My Shoes	70
Statement of Enlightenment 17	72
Title #18: It's True	73
Statement of Enlightenment 18	75
Title #19: Not Alone	76
Statement of Enlightenment 19	78
Title #20: Angel's Everywhere	79
Statement of Enlightenment 20	81
Title #21: The War	82
Statement of Enlightenment 21	84
Title #22: In Touch	85
Statement of Enlightenment 22	87

Title	Page
Title #23: Another Day	88
Statement of Enlightenment 23	90
Title #24: Storm Chaser	91
Statement of Enlightenment 24	93
Title #25: Seeds	95
Statement of Enlightenment 25	97
Title #26: Reach Out	98
Statement of Enlightenment 26	100
Title #27: Why Can't You	101
Statement of Enlightenment 27	103
Title #28: Pandora's Box	104
Statement of Enlightenment 28	106
Title #29: Fear For You	107
Statement of Enlightenment 29	109
Title #30: Northwest	111
Statement of Enlightenment 30	113
Title #31: Who's The Fool?	115
Statement of Enlightenment 31	117
Title #32: Dead Weight	119
Statement of Enlightenment 32	121
Title #33: Lady By The Bus	122
Statement of Enlightenment 33	124
Title #34: Mine	126
Statement of Enlightenment 34	129
Title #35: Character	131
Statement of Enlightenment 35	133

Title	Page
Title #36: Doomed	135
Statement of Enlightenment 36	137
Title #37: Reach Out	139
Statement of Enlightenment 37	141
Title #38: Rise & Fall	143
Statement of Enlightenment 38	145
Title #39: Cherish	146
Statement of Enlightenment 39	148
Title #40: Agape	150
Statement of Enlightenment 40	152
Title #41: Circles	153
Statement of Enlightenment 41	155
Title #42: Ignorance	157
Statement of Enlightenment 42	159
Title #43: Killing Your Baby	161
Statement of Enlightenment 43	163
Title #44: Think About It	164
Statement of Enlightenment 44	166
Title #45: Were Pigs	167
Statement of Enlightenment 45	169
Title #46: Mr. Know It All	171
Statement of Enlightenment 46	173
Title #47: Sister	175
Statement of Enlightenment 47	178
Title #48: Please	180
Statement of Enlightenment 48	182

From Darkness To The Wonderful Light

Title	Page
Title #49: Institutionalized	183
Statement of Enlightenment 49	185
Title #50: Useless to You	187
Statement of Enlightenment 50	189
Title #51: There's Hope	190
Statement of Enlightenment 51	192
Title #52: Government Gangsters	194
Statement of Enlightenment 52	196
Title #53: Let Go	197
Statement of Enlightenment 53	199
Afterword	201
Order Forms	203/205
Notes	206

About The Author

I was born in small town in the Rio Grande Valley called Mercedes Texas. April 28, 1962 was the day God introduced me to this world. My parents are Pete Martinez and Jaunita Martinez. By the time I reached the age of 2, my parents had decided to go their separate ways. From my understanding, my father was not ready to settle down, whatever the reason was, they are relatively not that important today. But what I feel is the fact that it was the beginning of many of my insecurities, and anger issues. My mother had two other children that I was unaware of and would not find out about it until my later years. And I also later found out that one of my siblings had died under the hands of the neglectful acts of my grandmother (maternal). I have heard that it was a way of death that I am sure that Satan could appreciate. I had gone through the misfortune of having to deal with several stepfathers, most were abusive, all were distant. I remember at a very young age living with my grandparents on my father side, they were very sound and good people, although my grandfather scared the hell out of me, it did not take me long to find out that under his extremely rough exterior lied the most loving man that I have ever been blessed to know. At the age of 4, I was taken away to live with my mother and also met my new stepfather. At that time I was very naïve and accepted him with an open heart. The problem was, I was at that time merely my mothers' spic son. That was something that affected me a great deal. At a very young age I had learned to be seen as little as possible and to be heard less. Also shortly afterward was introduced to my older sister who had been living with my mothers, mother. (ya I know), but I leave it at my mother had no choice.

Her father had left her the same. My sister and I were very different. I feel that the biggest difference was that she was very angry and hurt, where as I was younger and did not have it in me to live with anger. Growing into my pre-teen years that all changed. Being fed up with getting beat by my sister and dealing with the different forms of abuse that I would get from those that were feeding me; I started to change, and not for the better. People could not and would not hurt me, mentally or physically. I was growing up and thought that it was my time to be the one who did unto others as was done to me. Some had made me able to with stand a great deal of physical pain and others had conditioned me to deal with mental pain. I had become a very numb young man, though it was not in my heart, it was strong in my mind, I soon turned into a person that would deliver twice as much pain than was given to me. I became numb! I had developed the attitude of not giving a shit about others, but worse of all that, I didn't care about myself in any way. Not; a good way to live! At 15, I had hitch hiked to Detroit, Michigan to live with my father. That worked out for about 2 years. The time I was in Detroit, Michigan, I found that it only fed the negative thoughts and actions and I was doing good enough, I was given the reins to guide myself, (which is not something that I needed by a long shot). When I met with father, he had subjected me to an upper white middle class school in the suburbs. Not Bad, but I was the only minority at the school. There were no African Americans, no Asians, no Hispanics, I was a social outcast that had 99 pounds and crutches backing my spic butt up in a new place. Being one that was used to being the underdog, also one who had been through more trails than most my age, I became very violent and extreme with everything that I did. Not being accepted by most of my peers, I did find acceptance with a small percentage of people that were also outcast. Witnessing my father's behavior with alcohol, women and violence along with my new friends, I set my ways to be the best of all of this negative behavior. And I soon was with problems that I caused, along with not wanting to humble my actions, I started staying in the streets of Detroit. During that time I met what might be the best person who ever became part of my life, (Grams) a 60 + elderly woman that opened her home and heart to me. She was the first person that ever slapped the shit out of me for the soul purpose of letting me know she was worried about me. That did it; I was instantly committed to being the best person that I could be. It was the first time I had felt that anyone really cared about me along with my faults. I had been 16, living in her basement, when one unfortunate night she had a heart attack, she died for a brief moment, but I did manage to save her life, which was saving mine at the time. I was blessed enough to be able to then take care of her for a little more than 2 years; best 2 years of my life. I miss her, when she did pass on she had left her 2 story flat to me, to disgusted with her immediate family hearts and heads. I decided that they could shove it, the house meant nothing, Grams did and now she is gone. I had soon gone back to school, blew up my locker, and thumbed it to Texas with my mother to finish my last year of school. Again I felt alone and being Hispanic and going to an all Hispanic school you might think that I would fit in, but WRONG! I was the only one at the school that did not speak Spanish, again I was fighting getting drunk, doing drugs on a regular basis. Stealing cars breaking into homes, beating people was just part of ordinary day's activities. I had also started dealing drugs with my sister being one who opened that door for me, I became someone with the illusion of power and money, it did not last. I had ended up shooting a man for a deal gone wrong then moved back to Detroit getting a job then marrying my first real love. Kathy, when I got back with her she had already had a child that I also fell in love with (Nicole) followed with a child of our would do anything for my family, and was asked our own (Peter). I had loved my family along with all of my in-laws. Times were rough so I found the only solution was to go into the military. It took over a year to get excepted due to my juvenile record. Taking my family to Texas for the time while waiting to go in the army. They met my family. I had finally got the opportunity to go on. I did score well with my test, which gave me the choice to enter the officer training course, but I was not so smart, I enlisted as a combat engineer, air assault, and stationed to an airborne unit. I under gone many problems along with 2 adultery charges. If my drugs use, or violence did not manage to trip me up, the women did. I soon got discharged for misconduct pattern of misconduct, though it was under honorable conditions. With what I had saved along with in-laws help, my family and I purchased a house in the suburbs. I had felt that I was doing all that I could and did not feel that my other half was not doing the same, I left with clothes on my back and an old beat van. "The biggest mistake in my life". There I went, back to Texas, dealing many pounds of marijuana to Louisiana. Around that time I was also doing acid and cocaine. It did not take to long before I was out of control. I soon went back to Detroit where I became a cocaine dealer off of 8 mile. Not long back I met a young lady that was very attractive and had genuine innocence. Three months into our relationship, we had our first baby (Anita) she was the most important thing in my life. The day she came home I had put away my gun along with my drug dealing; I wanted nothing to happen to her. Ten months later we had a boy (Joe), I now had 2 people in my life that I would give up my soul to save them. I then needed a way to support them without endangering them also. So, I got into a apprentice program as an iron worker at local 292. Not being too happy with my home life,(not due to my children) I started using drugs again in the form of crack. I did stay functional for quite a few years, then came along my third child(Bianca).Which I loved just as much not long after Bianca came, their mother's sister developed cancer. I to move back to Detroit so that their mother could be close to her sister,(second biggest mistake). Work was not there, and along with putting up with the drunken ignorance of herself along with her family, I found more peace running the streets doing crack and whatever else went with it. I had found a genuine disgust of the very site of their mother's hygiene, attitude, drunkenness and that along with her brothers and sisters. Overdosing, getting shot at, and dealing with the streets were welcome more than dealing with the family that I was dealing with. As much as it hurt me I stayed with my family for two years without even sleeping with my children's mother. I solely to be close to my children and to make sure they were clean and doing good in school, I took to the streets full time, I became a full blown crack head. I fought in parking lots for a couple years for money, overdosed over 20 times, came closer to suicide than I care for, in and out of rehabs for depression drugs and violence. For some years I slept where I could and ate whatever I found,. Jails were a blessing. Throughout all of this I did not feel bad for myself, I felt bad for my children, and those that were in similar way of life I was living. So during all of this I started to put my life experience on paper. Through all of this I have found GOD in my life. Though my mother got murdered, father disowned me; my children don't know about me today, I am fine. I wish the best for everyone. And will do what I can for all those that I cross paths with. Today I can look in the mirror and say with honesty that I love who I am and I know GOD loves me more. LIFE IS GOOD!

Foreword

My thanks go to GOD, and GOD alone. For he has never forsaken me even when my back was turned, for the beautiful children that he has given me. For the people that he works in and that he has put in my path, for the times when I hungered to show me that I wouldn't starve for the times I felt abandonment to show me his presence for the times of sorrow to show me there's love, for the walks through my darkness, so I could learn of his light. For the torcher of demons, to gain some insight. For his giving his son, so that I can live. For his love and acceptance of all of my faults and short comings. And I thank him for giving me the opportunity to help others whatever way that I can.

Your journey will be one of hope, joy, sadness and enlightenment. I hope that you get as much out of From Darkness to the Wonderful
Light. You will be _____ .... Now, fill in the blank.

Acknowledgments

I dedicate this book to everyone who has hit rock bottom in life, to those who do not know of the Lord, and feel they are ready to just give up, and I have only one to thank, that is God himself. For without being able to reach out to God, I may never have been able to pull out of this dark life I was living. Many people that I have met never come out of what I was living like. I have witnessed many give up on life, and quite a few die in sin. I have seen a great beauty that lives in some and in others an ugliness that only Satan could appreciate. I was one of which I speak of, and am so thankful that the Lord blessed me with the will, faith, compassion and love for myself and others the same. Then I must be thankful to my children – Anita, Joseph and Bianca Martinez, they were the only ones of flesh that never did deny me. They gave me a reason to want to strive on, without them I feel I would not have lived long enough to find out how great God is. I am thankful for every trail and tribulation that I have went through, for they were all handed to me for a reason, I feel that that reason was to be able to humble myself and hopefully help others through the pains that I have endured. I pray that those who read this book, may find God and realize that there is a reason that God has you in your position, no matter what it is. And that everyone, in their own way is one of God's special children. He alone knows what you need in life and what you must go through. He is calling, and I feel that he wants all to invite him into their hearts and souls. And when I finally realized this, that's when I became alive. For I was one with an inner numbness that I can't describe enough; I am not saying that I am perfect by any means. And I don't think that God expects me to be, he does know that I am while on this earth, burdened with carrying this flesh of mine, I feel that for me to be as one, or be whole; that I must live my days on earth with a peace in myself. That means that the spirit and flesh must live in harmony, just as I have found out that I cannot live solely on feeding the flesh. I have also come to believe that the spirit must throw the flesh a bone now and then. Many believe different, and that's just fine. I do not burden myself with what any man condemns me of. My glory goes to God, and I know that he is pleased as we all know that even Jesus was not accepted by all. So by no means do I expect all to except me. I do not judge any man, God's judgment alone is what is important to me. Again, I am only a man, but one who has found happiness, compassion, love and an inner peace that is only possible though our Lord and savior. My relationship is a one on one basis. I will not allow anything or anyone to get in the middle of myself and God. And I will be thankful for one more thing, that is if at least one person that reads this book, finds the Lord.

Disclaimer

This Document is produced to help the reader and them insight into the purpose and demeanor of the poetic verses provided. The attached information is given by the author in an effort to provide the reader with a sense of the author's driving motives and the wonder of words through this written document.

The author's purpose for writing this book was directly related to his hills and valleys travel from darkness to the wonderful light. All the description, words and other information included were all original comments and not reprints from other sources.

You are invited to read this document in its entirety, which will be my hope that you are moved to take whatever actions you are led to by the Holy Spirit. I feel that the information in this book will in some way give you a better and deeper understand of life and the weaknesses you may experience from your rapid journey and it may satisfy what you are looking for as a personal need.

I have tried to eliminate the mistakes often made in this type of printed material. There may be some minor typographical and content errors. I do apologize if this occurs.

The other purpose of this book is to educate and give you food for thought. The author and publisher shall have neither liability nor responsibility to any person or entity with respect to any problems or damage caused, or alleged to have been caused, directly or indirectly, by the information provide within.

Introduction

Within the proper limits of an introduction it would be impossible to give any adequate summary of the literature with which these life involved poems are written. There are many that are familiar with many of the title written about. During this period of my life, I remember that a broken promise has very little power. Where there is fear and unbelief there is Sin. I know from firsthand accounts that

one must remain in control of their mind, body and soul to conquer those evil demons that reside in most of us.

Of all the problems, one may experience in their life it is most important that we foster absolute independence but remain forthright in all our endeavors. There is an old saying, "That life is a bitch and then you die."

God through Jesus has brought me constantly in contact with my own reality and has bought stability to my life and my travels through this life.

In this book, I have attempted to become a poet through my years of developing into the person I am today.

In most of my writing of poetry, I have added my own style of writing that is new to these modern ways of delivering a message. Literature has not quite died, at least not yet. I have to finish what I have started, ever thought I have fell on bad and hard times from time to time. My poems have been written entirely on my life experiences; that is not void of human and godly inspirations.

Title #1

Beware

Some use the LORDS name to Evangelize

There false Christian way.

So many are blind but hear every word

that they say.

Some may preach from the Bible

With strength and powerful voice.

They get praise from so many

that is why they rejoice.

From Darkness To The Wonderful Light

Some religion that is preached

Behind is a tool that is used. From the podium that's

preached from Gods' words are abused.

They may have a soft look

Or seen by many as pure.

They use the look of their flesh

Not there heart as a lure.

They may be fishers of men,

But they fish for their own gain.

reel a man in, It's his soul that is slain.

And it's a terrible shame some put

themselves on a throne.

When judgment day comes upon them,

From their seat they'll be thrown.

It is something real sad,

When the blind are led by the blind.

I pray for them both,

And that the Lord they will find.

So I pray that more people praise God

And his word.

And recognize the false Christian,

Know that he is absurd

Statement of Enlightenment 1

Let me just mention Rev. Jim Jones, and the ungodly incident at Jones Town. I am not saying that all legalism is to this devastating level, but legalism is legalism, in the same since what's Black is Black and what White it is White. So many who minister or preach, use only parts of the bible that suits them. For instance the bible says that God wants us to prosper. Does that mean that because you speak of God's words that you should be driving a Bentley on the profit of evangelizing. Whereas those that speak the word should act as if they are God's themselves. I am not saying that all should be as Jesus was, with not much more than a pair of sandals for his feet. What I am saying is that I have witnessed many who treat working for God as a worldly business. Only to fatten themselves up on these followers who are blind that give through necks, while thinking that they can buy their way to heaven, and I am not just specifically speaking of money. How many times have you heard of some who speak behind a podium to find out they have molested of committed sins that we may not even heard of. And I have seen churches that you're not up to their standards enough to be part of their congregation, and if you give to my church, I'll make sure you get into heaven" it's the only way, what a crock! God does want us to be prosperous, but I don't think he likes glutany, and sure we should give more to our brothers and sisters. Time, encouragement, love, Fellowship and godly spirit, those that give in all these ways is what I feel God wants as far as the takers of everything for profit, I don't know!

21

Title #2

CHANGING THE WORLD

You are changing the world every woken moment of the
day, with your actions your jesters or something you
say When you encounter a man-say you give him a
smile,
You just may have helped him lose a thought that was vile

From Darkness To The Wonderful Light

Another you pass may see hate on your face, you just
May have tainted a heart full of grace

Say you take from a man-who has little to nothing that
same night he may hunger, now isn't that something

If you're so full of hatred and you take a man's life well
there you fool, you just hurt his children and wife

If you throw a stone in a pond, all the waters affected
I hope your no stone, or there's lives you're afflicted

You are changing the world; you are changing your
Fate Will you end up in heaven, or in front of hells gate

I sure wish the best for you, I don't want the worst
I hope your soul lives on when your body lies in a

hearse, You are very important, your actions cause many

shifts you're important to this world, you are one of

GOD'S gifts

Statement of Enlightenment 2

This poem is very self-explanatory; it is so simple and so true. But why do we keep spreading a deep ugliness like a very contagious plague. God and the devil both are in a very serious conflict. God wants us to go to him on our own free will, whereas the devil will coax you, he will plant ugliness in a man's heart, whenever he can, and afterward it will spread to others instantly upon contact with another brother or sister, that is unless the person encountered is one of the Lord. If he truly is, he will take the ugliness and pass a little love instead. And hopefully the one he passed love to will in turn do the same. I want everyone to take a good look at thereselves and realize that you are a powerful being. You do have the power to change the world; it has to start somewhere, why not with you? And it is up to you on how you change it, Will you help shed darkness or will you spread a little sunshine. Whatever you do, it is your choice. And with what you choose will determine your fate when your bones are lifeless. Your soul may live in glory for eternity. Please remember that you are very special and you affect everybody and everything that you come in contact with. And from what I have witnessed in my journeys, is that there is a big need to change for the better.

Title #3

FREE YOURSELF

GOD Works in many, so many people they claim
often forgetting the day that Jesus was slain

Stones were thrown at our Savior, GOD must have been
crying
I'm sure the devil was pleased, as he saw GOD's son
dying

Jesus spoke to his Father, to spare all their lives
it is merely the devil that fills them with lies

Father, I know you could save me, but please save

From Darkness To The Wonderful Light

mankind

so many can't see, they are lead; they are blind

So if Jesus forgave the hate in so many others

won't you forgive your sisters and brothers

And if Forgiving is something, that's a hard thing to do

remember it hurts, the spirit GOD has in you

So whatever the case, please forgive from the heart

Please do it now, it's time to start

Statement of Enlightenment 3

Can you imagine where you would be if Jesus did not ask the father to forgive man while he hung on the cross, whipped, and given vinegar instead of water to quench his thirst? GOD could have wiped out the earth in its entirety, if it were not for Jesus asking for forgiveness of what man was doing to him. There are many today that can't forgive another for the cost of a dollar, a cruel word, or a simple, "well so & so said this." People get a hatred in themselves over something as stupid as here say. I've never seen anything good come out of revenge, or a spiteful act. Holding a grudge hurts those that it is upon and the one holding it. It is a senseless weight that one carries when they can't find it in their heart to forgive. When one learn to forgive others, only then you can start forgiving yourself. And as we all know that we may never forget, yeah that's right. Remembering and forgetting is involuntary, your mind either remembers or it doesn't. But, as far as forgiving, now that you do have control of it's not through your mind, but through the heart that we can forgive. They say a mind is a terrible thing to waste, well so are the good feelings of your heart. There are far more positive things to work on than to burden yourself with problems of he said, she said, he did, she did. Just let it go!! Give someone a break. More important, give yourself a break, hate, animosity, and ill will, are killers. Though they may not hurt your flesh, they will do quite a job on your heart and soul. Why not forgive someone, RIGHT NOW!

Title #4

Giving Thanks

I'm entitled to nothing, for what seeds I have sowed

I am thankful for what you give I have nothing owed

I have recently lost my home and new car

But I thank you for my legs, they'll carry me far

I thank you for every breath that you give to me

And for giving your son, that is why I am free

I thank you for the love that you keep in my heart

From Darkness To The Wonderful Light

And for the times I would stray. and you never did part

For the times when I fell, and felt a sense of despair

You always were there, to lift me up in the air

Trials and tribulations, yes; I give thanks for this to

They help get stronger, and closer to you

When I hunger you always, give food that is fresh

I thank you again; you feed my soul and my flesh

You have given me wants, and all that I need

I just ask and it's there, never having to plead

For the blessing you put, right in front of my face

Sometimes not deserving, I thank you for your grace

For the Christians around me, it is you that they love

And for the faith that you give, to be with you up

above The thanks that I have cannot be shown from a pen

So, I'll try to walk Christ like, do the best that I can

Statement of Enlightenment 4

So many of us feel that we are owed in everything that is part of our lives. Owed from your bosses, your family, friends, the government, and God. And many only find one day a year to be thankful, that is on Thanksgiving Day. Well, I'm here to tell you that you should be thankful every day of the year. Even through my times of desperation and total devastation. At first when I had lost everything precious in life and became isolated from society. I did feel that I had gotten the shaft. I felt that this reaction was normal, and though it may be. I have found that with every action there was a reaction in my life. And I feel that the reaction was one that the Lord had wanted me to witness. I also know that I have reached a sense of humbleness that I did not think was possible. I have also learned not to question the obstacles that are put in front of me. For many of them may have detoured me to something great, what if there was no obstacles I may have gone right past it, (The Blessing). I thank God for my hard times, for they have made me stronger. I thank GOD for the good times, for they help me keep faith that they will be there again. This poem was written after I had no doubt in my mind that I was saved, for a few years. I had been speaking to many on how blessed I have become and planted many seeds for the Lord, telling them of his glory. I feel that GOD owes me nothing. He already gave his son's life for me, so that I could live, and I also have a promise that he will not forsake me, along with the promise of being with him in heaven, an eternal life of paradise, and talk can sometimes be cheap, so I am one that will show my thanks through the way that I live.

Title #5

JESUS

There's a man at the corner, He holds a sign in the air.
Many drive by him, with no concern they don't care.

The sign says he's hungry. He could use some cash or
some food, Some people glance elsewhere, some may yell
something rude.

From Darkness To The Wonderful Light

The people don't know him, or care that he's down on
his knees, Is he a Christian or veteran, does he hold some
degrees.

He has swallowed his pride; he begs just to live, A Kick
While he's down are what most people give.

He may even lost loved ones, a child, a wife, but he is
Still judged, When they know not if his life.

If this man you give money, and he buys a drink or a
drug, at least it bought comfort; he has no one to hug.

If you won't reach in your pocket, or spare any change,
Maybe it's your life, which you need to arrange.

I'm asking you one thing, don't you point don't you
laugh, That man with the sign may be the lord with no
staff.

Statement of Enlightenment 5

We have a major problem here in our own front yard, here in America. That is homelessness. Though, I was one who was homeless for a long period of time. I Have not written this poem in reflection of my own life. I was one who walked into it, on my own free will, where as many have had devastating factors in their lives that have thrown them into the streets. I myself have met so many of them who are intelligent, God fearing, and just plain out great people, others lack skills, ambition or have just given up. But, no matter what the problem was that hurled them to this state. The common phrase is their just bums, who need to be shot. Judged so quick by those who haven't a clue about one's life. They are just like the rest of society, good, bad, smart, stupid, arrogant, Christian and followers of the devil. The one thing that is different as a whole is they don't have a home if more people took the time to find out a little more about Jesus. They may find that he was a man without a home. He performed miracles in the streets. And let me tell you, God lives in all, not in just those who have homes. I, myself am one to give a few dollars to those that ask, if I have it, and I am not starving, why not? It is not my concern of what they do with the money that I give. That is between the individual and God. Who am I to say what that man needs? I'll tell you another thing, several times I was given money and went straight to the bar or crack house.
Through someone's compassion and having a giving heart, they may have gotten the idea out of my head to kill myself or someone else for the money. Many

times I didn't need a sandwich, what I needed was something to help ease the pain in my heart and head. Who knows, I might not be alive today if it were not for someone giving me a few dollars. I may have went as far to obtain it by taking it in a bad way.

Title #6

JUSTIFIED

You showed little to no regard for a man Who had died

No-one cared for your life, so you feel Justified

You walked away from loved ones, at night children

cried but you were never nurtured, so for this your

Justified You've stole from your brothers,

Left many high and dry You were a poor deprived child,

So this you justify You've beaten down people,

From Darkness To The Wonderful Light

Walked away left them lie As a child abused yourself,

another action

Justified You've been untruthful to others,

To many you've lied You felt sheltered as a child,

Another justified You've drank away your life,

This you can't hide Your father was an alcoholic,

This you justified God tried speaking to you,

Oh how he tried and he tried So if you're not let up in

Heaven,

I guess he's justified.

Statement of Enlightenment 6

Wow! This describes myself to a tee, at one time in my life, I had an excuse for everything, I done so many wrongs, But I truly believed that I had a genuine justification for everything. All I can say is that I was walking this earth like a true abomination. Facts were that if someone did it to me, I had good reasons to do the same to the next person. What a fool! I certainty was not one to turn the other cheek; self-pity has a lot to do with my justifications. But the true problem was that I didn't know very much about Jesus. I certainty had no interest in reaching out to GOD, even though his arms have always been held wide open waiting for me. And sure what I have written has dealt with my life on a first hand base's. But, I finally opened my eyes and found out about the Lord. And when I became saved, a huge light went on. And then I realized, what kind of man would I be if I lived with the attitude, (Do unto other as they do unto you)? I started remembering how I had felt when these things had happened to me. And how I felt toward those that did this to me. And I do realize that the past is the past, and I cannot undo anything. But the one thing I can do is walk as Christ like as possible, stop doing wrong to others. So today I try to put myself in the other person's shoes and ask myself how I would like the actions that I am doing. I have found the Lord, I have repented and will not make excuses, the free will that I have is exactly that, free-will. No-one has made me do anything to anybody and I do pray that those I have done wrong to, that they please forgive me.

Title #7

Lost Then Found

I had lost something dear; it had brought me great

shame. You see I had played a dark gruesome game.

I had walked in such blindness, for so many years.

When I think of it now, it still brings me tears.

I didn't much care; I would treat it like dirt.

I had felt so much pain; I had felt so much hurt.

Many cold lonely days, so many cold lonely nights,

I held so much hatred, I fought so many fights.

From Darkness To The Wonderful Light

The battle I fought, one I sure couldn't win.

I would not surrender, and I wouldn't give in

The sad part was; that to win was to lose,

And not giving in is a bad choice to choose.

But I finally surrendered, put my hands in the air_

When I broke down I found, so much love so much

care,

You helped me dear lord, I have faith and a goal.

Thank you dear God, you have found my lost soul.

Statement of Enlightenment 7

I was born with a soul, along with the spirit of God in me. When I speak of the soul, I am referring to the spirit; the one, that God lives in us with. And I do believe that every living creature has a soul. The reason I say this because I have witness quite a few of them leave it's host upon death, it's an eerie sight. For many years I walked this earth as an empty host. Little to none as far as feelings are involved, it's what I had to do, put all feelings to the rear. After living like this so long I put my feelings in such a dark place that it was not that easy to find when I wanted it, a big empty hole that needed to be filled. I guess you could say I was like the Tin man in the wizard of OZ. I can't remember the last holiday of any sort where I spent it with someone, but that was ok, I was accustomed to being alone. I did so many wrongs to my brothers and sisters that it is pretty sad. Remorse was not part of my vocabulary, nor was God. Many people told me that there was something great in store for me. And all told me that I needed to find GOD and become a new person. Well that scared me a lot, I was afraid to lose the only person that I knew, I was scared of killing the one person that always there. I was afraid of putting an end to myself and who I was. If I surrendered to the lord, I never surrender to anything or anyone, (who would I be). Guess what? I did it; I surrendered and I'm still me. And thanks to the lord I am now a better me with no more lonely times, fights, and tears with myself. There was never a reason to be afraid to surrender.

Title #8

Sad Truth

Under a bridge there's a man there that sleeps Often at
night you can hear his cries and his weeps

This man he is beaten, he's dirty and foul

With his dealing's in life, he has thrown in the towel

He is also an addict, he'll put a drug in his vein It helps
all the hurt, it help's all his pain

In war he's seen death, a sight for sore eye's those are
some reason's some reasons he cries

From Darkness To The Wonderful Light

This man he has no-one, hated by all in his life His
mother, his father, his children, his wife

He's been beating by life, he's been beaten real bad
Accustomed to this, it is pretty sad

In the morning at church, he gets some milk and some
bread His belly gets full, but he has a pain in his head

He'll beg for some change, and look for some cans He'll
tote all that he can, in his big dirty hands

He will get some drugs with the change that he made.
Put the syringe in his vein, soon his pain will fade

When he nods out he'll dream, that his life is pure bliss
Reality's something that he surely won't miss

When the drug has worn off, you can see a tear in his
eye this feeling he hates, often wishing he'd die

Back at the church, to get some food for the night he
has tossed in the towel he has no more fight

This man manages to get, more drugs for his head now
he's back at the bridge, with cardboard for a bed

With the drug in his vein, he'll cry out and he'll weep
He prays LORD have mercy, don't let me wake from
my sleep

Statement of Enlightenment 8

Through the course of my life I have lived and seen this life style in myself and many others. Though I only a couple of times have put drugs in my veins. This poem reflects greatly on my own life for a period of time, the deaths that I have seen and been involved with were during my war that is still going on. Every day in our own streets people are being murdered for virtually nothing during my days in the streets, death was nothing out of the ordinary. But many times at night I would reflect on the things that I had seen, only to break down in a heavy remorse. Not having family and friends that I could ask for help, led me to sleeping where ever I could. The feelings of hopelessness lead to more drugs, drugs would help me to forget and at the same time kept me bound to the streets. After living like this for so long, it started getting easier that's how I accepted that, that is how it would remain. Again I have been told that man is not a being that is meant to be alone. So there were many nights that I would go to sleep where ever I was, with a tear in my eye, wishing that I would not wake up Only to start another day in the same way. This poem is the sad truth and I am blessed to have experienced it and more blessed by the lord to be out of it. But let me say there are many others that are still out there and today I pray to God to pull them out like he has pulled me out. Another truth is that many will not grab God's hand when it is held out and so many will die in their misery. Again I thank the lord for his mercy on me.

Title #9

REMEMBERING

I pray for the people, the ones who rob and they steal
they are robbing themselves; it's with the devil they
deal

The ones with hard hearts, yes I pray for their soul
the devil he holds it, there life must take a toll

For complainers and whiners, for the feel they are
owed

From Darkness To The Wonderful Light

its enlightenment they need, the walk down Calvary

road And for the ones who blaspheme, or they ridicule

you

Please lord forgive them, they know not what they do

Please bless those in darkness, they don't know of your light

At least give me the power, to pass others insight

And bless the ones with addictions, the ones the devil has

bound I pray that one day; it is you that is found

And please bless the ones, the ones I know prayed for me

Thanks for answering their prayer, now I'm one who can

see.

Statement of Enlightenment 9

I am one that believes that GOD hears every genuine prayer that is presented to him in true honesty and humbleness. But I am also told that the prayers of a true righteous man are very powerful. I was a person in a real desperate part of my life I was all of these things and more. Though often I prayed to the lord to pull me out of this darkness. Many people do and always will, its funny how in the mist of self-destruction or the feeling of doom is when everyone seeks the lord. I know I did. But I can honestly say I did this only out of desperation. And when I was in my comfort I would forget about God. Yes, I was bound, and to unbind myself was something that seemed impossible. There were some people that were truly of God that I have had the pleasure of meeting with and exchanging feelings. And I'm being one who would admit my deepest problem's to a person that was willing to listen was not very hard for me to do. Well I know that there must be a, righteous man out there that along with myself must of asked God to take a second look at my heart. Well, I do thank those that saw a small light in me and helped me get out of the darkness. So in turn, I do pray for those that are in the place in their lives that I was. I think it would be very selfish of me to let God pull me up and not try to pull up anyone with me. Kind of like that game, (a barrel of monkeys). I never will forget of the time in my life where I was one that needed help and fellowship. Again I thank the Lord for putting some of his children in my path.

Title #10

SELFISH

For the boy who feels lost, often cries for his dad

He got up and left, it hurt this boy pretty bad.

Will he grow up successful or fall into the street

who knows with no father to put a belt to his seat?

Mom is right there, she plays both the parents it's true

she struggles alone, does anything she has to.

She misses her man, but he doesn't love her.

He left so fast, it was just a big blur

this man he chose drugs, that's just how it is

the concern he has in life. Alone it is his

He wants freedom, no boundaries, no matter

What be the cost

You see it's more important,

Than the loved ones he's lost

His father left him, so to him it's ok.

But deep down inside, He wanted to stay.

I feel sorry for the man who

is living this life

but mostly feel sorry for that lonely

boy and poor wife.

Statement of Enlightenment 10

Yes, this written first hand on what I have done. I was a young man of about 20 years of age when I first got married. I was violent, though not to my family, not saying that I didn't hurt them. I know I did, and in a big way. I have no legitimate reason. I could point a finger at what started the domino effect, but I won't I was an immature young man who was not satisfied with anything, though at first I did give it my best shot, the family thing. But, I did find excuses to walk away in my own selfishness. Yes, it is obvious that I hurt myself. I still love my first wife and always will, and as far as my son goes, I love him the same. As the fool that I was, I was not strong enough or selfless enough to stop the domino effect that has went on in my life as a child. I was a boy who had no boundaries or limits. And I had felt the since of being bounded, I was used to drugs, violence, girls, adventure and so many more things that I didn't give myself a chance to experience a normal family life. I never had it so I never realized what I was missing I hope that one day that they can find it in their hearts to forgive me. In their eyes I may not be worthy of forgiveness. I am solely responsible for not breaking the cycle, and if my son and ex-wife don't forgive me. I at least pray that my son is a better man than I was, and he breaks the cycle. Two wrongs don't make a right, and through my selfishness, I did the second wrong.

Title #11

Shell of What Was

Up and down the streets again; on this you surly can

depend She's looking for a man to date; Street lights

are on

its very late She doesn't care about her life; she knows

she'll never be a wife, She'll please a man for a little

change, her life she surly must arrange.

From Darkness To The Wonderful Light

The man doesn't care about her pain, the lack of love it is Insane. She hurts real bad sometimes shell cry so many times, she wants to die This woman she is just a shell of who she was, Right here, her hell Shell go back home, no one to hug. She's hurting — but she has her drug. She'll take the money that she made, then shoot black tar — her pain will fade. Shell nod out quick - she may O.D. It's Heaven that - she hope's she'll see.

Statement of Enlightenment 11

How sad it is when a beautiful child of God stops loving themselves, and in turn no one else shows her love or compassion. Women in many cases treat themselves like something that should be flushed down the toilet. Many prostitute themselves out for necessity, be it money, drugs, or a sense of worthlessness. These are the women that I pray that one day they find help through the Lord. Then there are those that prostitute themselves out for the pleasure of it. I don't have much to say about that, with free will and a mutual consentment, I feel that it is not right, but I do not judge – when living in the streets I have befriended many prostitutes. Not solely to take advantage, I am not one to use a women though there have been cases when I have had intercourse, but not for money or favor. Many women are treated like dirt, and they are excepting of it. What a shame, I have had the pleasure of befriending several prostitutes that had a bigger problem or bigger (problems), No family, banished, or no other means in their heart or mind to survive any other way. I have also lost some dear friends this way. A couple of them had died from an overdose of drugs. Another just came up dead, with no excuse. But, what a shame, they had a beauty in them that most others didn't see. That most others didn't want to see, let me say this, I have two daughters, and they are doing very well and following the Lord in a very big way. Neither of them drinks, smokes, does drugs, or are free with their body's. I am blessed. But, if, And I pray it never happens, and I don't think it will, if they fell into prostitution, it would be tearing my heart apart to think of the lack of love they had for themselves or more so the way they are treated by society.

Title #12

WHO'S GAME

This is to you, if you think you such a bad ass

the devil may school you, you don't want his class

At one time in life, I had somewhat of a tail

I destroyed all that was good, I never did fail

I had plenty of money; in every corner a whore

I'd always say bluntly, "I'm the one I adore"

I gave GOD no credit, the devil, he was the one

From Darkness To The Wonderful Light

To rape pillage and burn, that was sure fun.

I was even so stupid to tell men time and again,

"If you want to dance with the devil, well let us begin,

I thought even at one time, I ruled this here world,

some nervous at my sight, some puked and they

hurled. I'd laugh at the fools; I'd laugh with great

pride. I had the devil so in me, there's nothing I'd hide.

I know quite a few times, the LORD tried speaking to

me, I was a possessed hateful monster, would not bow

to one knee, angered the LORD so, several times

getting cut lose He gave me the rope, and I made one

hell of a noose. Those times that he let go, I was

raped, pillage and burned Demons had got me, in a

short time I learned

So if playing with the devil, is one thing you do,

believe me you fool, he's playing with you.

Statement of Enlightenment 12

I was my own highest power: what a fool I was. I felt hat every person that I knew was weaker than I was. I don't just mean in brute strength I am talking about the whole nine yards of what make a man up. I had a leadership quality that was one that I would take, I treated everyone as my inferior. I would make men and women the same (cry) for I was the one who broke down spirits and belittled all. I would take risk like no other and put myself in situations that would make most buckle at the knees with fear. I remember a time which lasted a hell of a long time, where I would walk down the street and laugh, and seeing everyone close their doors as I passed, feared me. That gave me a great sense of power; I would also push drugs to the limit that would probably put the average horse down on the ground. I do know that crack cocaine is a serious drug that will separate you from God and lead ya right into the arms of the devil. Well, being one who never knows when enough is not enough I was let go by God or should I say, "I think that God wanted me to see what I was getting myself into. When he let the devil control parts of Job's life it was to prove a point to the devil, when God let the devil mess with me, it was to prove a point to the devil when God let the devil mess with me – Let me tell you " I had a small legion of demons all over me. I saw a glimpse of what hell can be like. I did realize, though it took a long time and it took a few trips to hell. But, I did find out that if you play with the devil, or play for the devil, you are a fool! If you want to play with him, just remember. (It's his ball) and he plays with you. Not the other way around.

Title #13

What I'll Say or Do

My mother My father My children My wife, Just a few of
The people that I've loved in life

The sad part about it is, Most are not here
There flesh may be buried, but I still hold them dear

Some of the people may have thrown me away
Appalled by my sight, I guess you could say

Others they Love me, but don't like all of my ways

From Darkness To The Wonderful Light

Their always wishing for me better days

Others' scorned, cause I can't walk by their side
So their feelings of love for me, they often do hide

For many it's hard to love and forgive
But I know that's just how the Lord wants me to live

Some may be baffled, they may call me a fool but I
sure believe, that it's God's golden rule

Sometimes I anger, I'm only human at best
But I soon shed the darkness, give hate a quick rest

Some they may die, with hate heavy at heart please
don't do this, it will tear you apart

In the next life , I wonder how many I'll know, I hope I
see all I loved , I hope this is so

I guess this won't happen, I don't feel it to be. So I
pray to you Lord, Forgive all not just me.

If we all make it to heaven, I'd sure like it that way
To all of my loved ones hears a few things that I'll say

My father may cry, for wishing me dead
I won't say too much, I'll just hug him instead

For my mother's neglect, she may claims she's insane
I'll just tell her I love her and help ease her pain

From Darkness To The Wonderful Light

My wife she may say, she knows he was spiteful! I'll
tell her I love her, and she sure was a sight full

and if I've done for my children, what the Lord wanted of
me, we'll have little to say, we'll just hug for eternity Lord,
this you will see.

Statement of Enlightenment 13

This is hard to explain, for the fact that those who did put a heavy pain on my heart, I do understand and forgive. I speak of my Mother's neglect, which is not her fault or was it her intension. She was a single Mother who tried to make sure that I was fed. The downfall was that she had to wait on whatever man she was with to be the bread maker. Much of her attention went to my step-Father and my younger half-sister. I was the fourth of fifth wheel along with my older half-sister. I was a child that required little attention and my Mother thought of me as her independent little man. It was not the case, but I did play the part well, even at a young age. I do feel she did the best she could and I loved her tremendously. As for my Father, I remember as a child being his pride and joy, with a condition though, that was to be exactly like him, minus the partying. A very smart man with many double standards. He did the best he could. I feel that his banishing of me was a great deal my fault. I was on crack for a while and made bad choices. I chose to be an individual and did not take his advice. So, I followed a different path. He knew that I had potential to be more like him. But, the truth of it all is I like being me. Though it gets hard I have learned more about life than many that I know, even if it was the hard way, (it was my way). I do not blame my Father, for not talking to me; I just hope that before his last day comes that his heart will soften. For his own good and mine, as far as the Mother of my children, I feel a great deal of pity for her. I did love the family life and had a love for her, but I was not in love with her and family. The Kayos that went along with her family were too much for me, I chose to be in the streets instead. Today, she is scorned and demonstrates a pure hatred toward me. I do not blame her. After I chose the streets, she would often hold the children against me that was very hard. Many times I would try to speak to her and the children only to have the door slammed in my face. I do feel bad for her and I hope that one day she will find an inner peace, that will take reaching out to God and I pray that she will someday. And then there are my children, the first born hasn't seen me since he was a young child. I do hope that he will find it in his heart to forgive me, I do have three others that I am very close to without them I might not have stayed alive to find God. They have been my inspiration just to keep breathing. Though they did not like my life style, they never stopped loving me. I must say, (there acceptance of me no matter what) is one of the best feelings that I could ever have. They are the sole one's that really knew that despite my exterior that inside the flesh there is a great spirit, and that has helped me through life. So bottom line, what I'm saying in this poem is that I have no hate or animosity in my heart today. And never really did. I do hope we all meet in paradise one day. And I do hope all can forgive me. If Jesus forgave while on the cross, why can't we all forgive for things that are nowhere close to that of which happened on Calvary road?

Title #14

Keep faith

Your body's a temple; it's the one that GOD gave,

Your spirit and soul will take this home to the grave.

So many will knock so beware of who you let in,

They may be sent from the lord, or the ruler of sin.

Some may bring hate or an abundance of love,

Beware though there not all with the Lord up above.

From Darkness To The Wonderful Light

Some show plenty of love, they may touch your heart,

But you don't know for sure, they may tare you apart.

Others may promise you fortune and *fame,*

Take caution again are you pawns in their game.

Some might say they might give up their life for you,

But the only one so far is, JESUS, it's true.

Your life will bring many so this I suggest,

Don't judge all too quick, treat them as a guest.

First use discernment, have some faith in mankind,

If you don't open the door, there's no goodness you'll

find. A monster maybe beautiful, it may be a disguise,

But the lord may send someone, not appealing to eyes.

A hard look a rough voice may hold a saint deep

Inside, And sometime in meekness the devil will hide.

So best I can say is have faith take a chance,

You never know who may enrich or enhance.

So don't lose your faith, or get a stone for a heart,

Remember the lord see's you, to me this is smart.

Statement of Enlightenment 14

It hurts me deeply to think of all of the people is have met through my journeys, that will not take a minute to urinate on you if you were on fire. So many people for so many reasons put up a wall with their brothers and sisters. Always quick to assume the worst in everyone. I have met so many that have a look of danger. But, when you take a minute to find out who they are under their skin. You can find many that are genuine good and Christian people. Then I have met those that walk with a Bible in one hand and the other hand a ready to strike you down. I have learned in my lifetime not to judge anyone to quick. I understand that to use caution is a sensible thing to do. But to shun everyone away without any reason but for the fact that they remind you of someone else who had hurt you in the past is ridiculous. If one Black, Brown or White man did you wrong. Surely doesn't mean they are all good or bad, we are all unique. How many people were of God that has been treated like they were leapers? Just because of quick judgment. (It is ashamed). There are still people out there that are not just out to hurt you. When you lose your faith in mankind doesn't that separate you from GOD?

Title #15

Limitless

I walk this world all alone, I do as I please this world is my oyster, Most things come with ease.
Along with no boundaries, none have shown much care, I'm somewhat of a monster, even I must beware.
I'm cunning I'm wise, I can poke anyone's eyes, It's my gift; it's my curse, its one I despise.
I will snap in a second, I've hurt many real bad,
When I've come to my senses, great remorse, I feel

64

sad. I've stepped on my family, and if I don't know
you, I may stomp on your life; I don't know what I'll
do.

I'm a sensitive person, if you pierce my heart,
I'm meek, I am violent, and you will meet one part.
If I walk away sadly, it only hurts me,
It's my violence, the part, I hope you don't see.
Right now in a place, with guidelines and rules, Upon
my release, I must use these tools.
In a very short time, be on top of the world,
But I will self-destruct, all good will be hurled.
I know it is wrong, I shouldn't say this, but it *never*
does fail, I never do miss.
Right now in the middle, I'm not up I'm not down, my
life is in shambles, am I a monster or clown.

Statement of Enlightenment 15

This was written during a time when I had put myself in rehab, and anger management. I was in a facility for about one month. I had bouncing in and out of such facilities for quite a while. Most of those times when I checked myself it was only to take a break for a while somewhat similar to a nass car pulling in to a pit stop just to get refueled and a new set of tires. Though, I was on top of my game in the streets. Somewhat, ahead in the race that the only victory was the checkered flag straight to hell. Being in the race for so long I managed to steer around every bump, crack or obstacle that got in my way. While in the facilities I did hold a genuine sorrow and shame for taking advantage of everyone just to get ahead. And I became quite good at it. I learned how to deceive, manipulate, and basically run over everyone in my way with a great ease, charm, wit and a smile that would win almost everyone that I met over. The few, and I do mean the few times that I could not win over with the gift of gab, I might strike out. And other times I would feel great shame from taking advantage of everything and everybody, not a single soul was safe from my hypnotizing ways. Being in rehab has always been my sanctuary. I was not eating out of garbage cans and living in abandon buildings or was I loaded with money from the pounds of marijuana that I used to sell. I do know one thing for sure, and that is that I was a very confused person. Angry and sad, or meek and violent, I know that it is contradicting but that is how I was. Again, no-one was safe, not even myself.

Title #16

Hardening

Here on the devils playground, the Lord is losing the war, It seems by a landslide but there's no way to keep score. Hardened hearts are all places, there's so many so vast. The devil he is winning, there's a huge darkness he's cast. So many people I've met, there so callused and cold, I feel were at the end of days, it's in the bible I'm told. It's getting much harder to keep my faith in mankind, becausewhen I look behind smiles, there' hardened hearts that I find. As a drowning man holds you under to stay on top to get air,

From Darkness To The Wonderful Light

Men step on others who are down; I see it every place,
everywhere.

When I looked at myself, I feel so different you see, I don't

step on others. I'm too busy stomping on me. Don't for one

second think you can step on me too, cause if you try this, I

surly will stomp on you. I'm surly not Jesus, or I wouldn't

think like this, There's so little in life; I find good or sense of

bliss. I have approached many people, planted millions of

seeds, But the soil in some hearts, nothing grows except

weeds. I'm so glad there's still a few that walked in gods

light. Their kind words or fellowship help my faith through

the night, when I meet those with good hearts, it touches

mine and it grows. Its helps me deal with evil, all the lashes

and blows. But there's a point where break down, I might

just lash out back, That the one thing that scares me, I

might go totally whack, I've been hurt many times, but I'm

accepting of this, I don't want to strike out, I may kill I

won't miss.

I reach out to the doctor's to help me gain some control,

They say it's the cocaine, it takes a terrible toll. So many

that walk are so hateful and mean, I don't like to lose

control, because then that's how I'm seen.

Statement of Enlightenment 16

I am told that earth is the domain of the devil that God gives him, or should say allows him some of this domain. From what I have witnessed I can see that the devil has hardened many of hearts. The sour looks and evil looks that you get from people can be piercing. Not to mention the snarly remarks that comes from so many. It does and always has took a toll on my own attitude – after being on the receiving end of the hardened ones, it sometimes gets over whelming and in turn puts a negative effect on my own attitude. Whereas then I am one that starts hardening myself. And I feel that I am harder on myself than anyone should be. I do except my problem and the torment that I put upon myself. But really, enough is enough, I don't need others beating me, I do a good enough job myself. Many times I have struck out at others for the smallest reason. I guess it's just like the straw that broke the camel's back. Nothing ever good comes at this point; I have physically hurt many, even those that were important in my life. And then all of the sudden, it's like God sends someone to me to fellowship with. He does know I listen very carefully and absorb everything that he is sending me. And then I am fine again. Without God in my life I know I would have totally snapped to the point of no return. And so many doctors have told me that my only problem was drugs. I find it to be just one of the symptoms from the big picture. But they are educated so they must know my problem. (Yeah Right!) So I pray often to the Lord to help me along with others not to become one who has developed a hardened heart.

Title #17

My Shoes

For years I've been wandering, some may call me a bum
I'm in the school of hard knocks, and I'm surely not
dumb
Some; they go to college, to obtain a medical degree
I to have diplomas, there the scars that you see
Some they may save lives; they may have a great skill
But if they had no choice giving, could they take; could
they kill, In some ways I've done both, I have took and

From Darkness To The Wonderful Light

I've given Self-preservation; the first rule, I know the lord; he's forgiven I have done many of things, just to live and survive All the bad that comes with good, it's not something I strive, many doctors are robbers, they may pull a plug But do you call these men thieves; do you call them a thug? I think not; I know not, this sure isn't the case If I do this for survival, I get shame and disgrace These words are for those, who think they're so holy and good, I am ok with my life, GOD; he knows where I've stood I know I am no better, but you may not be better than me I hope that you may look from my side whenever you see So please open your eyes, we are all children of GOD So if we ever cross paths, I hope you give a nod

Statement of Enlightenment 17

I have chosen to be a loner for many years of my life. I don't really know exactly why. "But I am". I think that a big part of it is due to my early years of having to fend for myself. I never felt that I could cry for help to much of my family or friends. I would often get myself in a bind. And when I did reach out, many times I would hear the familiar words "you got yourself in it, now get yourself out". Then in my later years I was one who many times had doors slam in my face. I had burnt almost every bridge that I ever had. And for many years I didn't realize that I had one that could not be brunt, and that was the one with God. I have done many wrongs to survive. And after a while I did many wrong due to my wants. I was out of control. I have beaten, robbed, disgraced many, but I felt that I had to many times just to eat. I am by far not a stupid man though I have done stupid things. I, by choice had put myself through a course of survival. And my mentality was that the strong will survive and the weak will get eaten. And many of those people I saw did many of the same wrongs. But, I saw others doing it with a cold heart, acts that were not out a necessity but for gain. When they needed not to, Today, I know that through Jesus that I am forgiven. Because it was a time that I was a product of man; and today I know that I am a product of God. And I also know that it is wrong for me or anyone to judge others. (That's God's job)

Title #18

It's True

Why be so hateful, why be so cold

You carry some misery, on your face it is told

You imprison your own self, surrounded by rage

The LORD'S not responsible; you put yourself in this

cage The LORD gave us free will, he's freed us; from

sin But if you reach to the LORD a new life may begin

The reason I say this, you may have demons inside

But if you pray to the LORD, there's no place they can

From Darkness To The Wonderful Light

hide Pray to the lord, for all darkness to fade

Walk into his light, not in Satan's shade

When you walk in his light, his warmth it feels great

The cold darkness will leave, along with the hate

I know this is true, I once had clinched fist

That was until; I walked in GOD"S mist

And don't get me wrong, you'll still find up's and

down's But you won't go through life, with so many

frowns And through the course of your life, you feel the

sense of quicksand, just pray to the LORD, he'll pull

you out with his hand for all this to work, you must

have faith and believe Our GOD is a true one; there are

no tricks up his sleeve

Statement of Enlightenment 18

This hits home, the demons of anger and rage were extremely strong, the held my heart and soul hostage. Though I always felt bad afterwards I was still one that was driven in an instant to hurt others, I was one who acted on impulse. Be it verbally or physically I would attack at the blink of an eye. What was even worse for me is that I walked with a heavy weight on my soul and mind. Though I was never one to hurt women, children or anyone that I felt was weaker than myself. I had a darkness that would wish great harm on many. I surely lived in misery. Then I started to seek out the Lord and beg for his help to make my life a little easier. So that maybe I could know what it felt like to smile a little in life. Well, through prayer and a genuine desire and will to lighten up on myself and the world, it started getting easier and easier to go through my days with a lighter heart, and a brighter smile. I started to realize that life was not half as bad as I thought that it was. Today my days are brighter and my nights are sound. I have come to believe that with God's help, and a strong faith, that life is good. Even when it looks like my face is in the dirt, that's ok. I will pick myself up and dust myself off, and though may face may hit the dirt, at least I'm not six feet under it. God's great to have in my life.

Title #19

Not Alone

My flesh walked alone, for so many of years
I got pretty lonely, sometimes I shed tears
My mother got murdered, in the most violent way
My father despised me, he had thrown me away
No brothers, no sisters, that's how I grew
To mostly depend on myself, to me nothing new
When I came or I went, no-one was aware
For the few times they noticed, they didn't much care

From Darkness To The Wonderful Light

]not accustom to having, any good in my life

I neglected this woman, pushed away my poor wife

pushing life many times, to fill a hole that I had

Overdosing, shot, stabbed, many times I've gone mad

I've been tortured by demons, stared hell in the face

When I looked at myself, I felt shame and disgrace

This death wish I had, I don't quite understand

I am breathing today, by the LORDS precious hand

Now being quite older, I've grown in many ways

I've lived a life for a few, in all of my days

Now a little bit wiser, there's something else that I see

I have three beautiful children, and the LORD next to

me

Statement of Enlightenment 19

As a young child I had always felt that I was a burden on others. Even with my parents, I had never felt that anyone cared of anything that I did. Even though I do have two sisters, they are sisters due to my mother's other men in her life. Being that they were half-sisters I didn't grow up with them. And the years that I did, it didn't seem very good. My older sister would make sport of beating on me physically and my younger sister would find a way for herself to have her Father and my Mother beat me verbally. I was the little Mexican middle child that was pushed from my Father then back to my Mother many times, depending on how long they could handle me in their lives. I in turn did the same; I had pushed away two wives and four children at one time in my life. I had felt not wanted as a child and became unaccustomed to being alone. (I was not happy) then later I didn't know how to handle being close to anyone. Through my misery, drugs had filled this hole, or the truth is that it had numbed my heart. I had felt worthless and was in a great deal of emotional pain. Drugs were the answer! I can't even begin to count how many times I overdosed and seen glimpse of hell and demons. While in an abandon truck in Florida, one night I decided to end life. That's when I started to remember the story of Job. I then chose not to take all the drugs that I know would have killed me and realized there must be a reason I'm still alive. Then I felt the Lord had spoken to me and three of my children loved me. Then the light went on! (I was not alone, never was and never will be) Thank God.

Title #20

Angel's Everywhere

Our life is similar to court; at least that's what I see,
When judgment day is upon you that will be the end of
your plea. Like in court there's a prosecutor who wants to
send you right to a cell, the devils just like this, he wants
to send you straight to hell. As a Lawyer pleas for you,
your honor this man needs a break, an angel just like this,
he'll speak to god "please lord forsake", so when
judgment is ruled, will see heaven or

hell, Well there my brother, the life your living will tell. Were you kind, were you loving, did you help all those that were in need? Or were you selfish and relentless with a heart full of greed, were you humble are you worthy, were you kind to all other men, or did you look down your nose at others so often time and again. Did you walk somewhat Christ like, did you have the lord in your heart, or were you just a false Christian with a heart sour and tart. Did you see with some insight, did you look at the hearts that were inside, or when you looked at a man did you just see flesh just his hide. I have a love for all people, when judgment days here I hope that you'll be ok, I hope there's an angel right by you, just like a lawyer, I pray.

Statement of Enlightenment 20

I had wrote this poem after I had become saved, and looked back at who the old me was. I feel that it's never too late to begin a new life, as long as you are breathing and can ask for forgiveness there is still hope for a beautiful eternal life. I also know from the depths of my heart that there are angels sent down by the Lord to look out and protect each and every one of us. I feel that they have pulled my flesh out of near death experiences but more important they have pulled my soul out of an eternal death situation. But in doing so they are also fighting the devils helpers. At one time I was on the side of the devil and treated my brothers and sisters as if they were dogs. My eyes were closed to anything that was good in anyone else. (I was Blind) was one with no insight. I know that when judgment day is here for me that the sins that I have committed on my brothers and sisters will be thrown out of court. Only because I believe that our Lord is merciful and that if you can repent and change your ways, that there is hope for your soul. And if you are not one to do this, I truly hope that your guardian angel will speak up and help the Lord look at you twice.

Title #21

The War

The flesh that I have, it's a ravenous one

It devourers all good, it never is done

My spirit it walks, with the lord up above

It hungers for peace, and plenty of love

I don't feed the flesh, but sometimes it takes

It tears me apart; I'm a monster it makes

The spirit I feed, with good acts and good deed's

From Darkness To The Wonderful Light

To get close to GOD, that is some of the needs

The war between both, nobody can see

But believe me it's true, it's tormenting me

I don't like my flesh, I wish it would die

Six feet in a grave, I wish it would lie

But my spirit it knows, I can't kill it, not that

cause hell is the place, that I will be at

And if the flesh that I have, dies accidently

Surely the lord, he will accept me

Suicides close, it gives me a scare

Surely hells where I'd go, I better beware.

So I go on thorough life, with this war that's in me,

I guess I will live, what will be it will be.

I didn't want to hurt you, or even myself,

The depression I have must be put on a shelf,

So I pray to you lord, please help me through life,

I feel like my heart, it holds a big knife.

Statement of Enlightenment 21

Just tired – That's the only way I can describe my life at one point every since I was a child I knew that it was a sin that I feel cannot be forgiven. But, I thought about it many of times. I felt that I had been the rope in a tug of war game between God and the devil. Most all of the life that I remember has been this way. I know what I should be like and I knew what I should not do. I always yearned for peace and love and a sense of happiness. But, then I also saw that long narrow path that has been and always will be the path that I want to walk. But, there is a but; that a pretty picture. The wants of my flesh are exactly what the devil offers me and in an abundance, lots of money, beautiful women, and power, and it is so easy to obtain these things, (but at what cost). I have always known that, and that is what made my life hell at one time. I only recently realized that long and steady pays off a lot more than short and now. The time that I was drugging heavily and whoring the same, sure the flesh was pleased. But damn! The pain that my heart and soul felt, even while the flesh was feeding, was unbearable, a very heavy guilt and remorse. But, there I go again; I get over it and do the exact same thing that was going to hurt my heart once again. So many nights I cried out to the Lord to strengthen me and it seemed that every morning that it was the devil that woke me up in the morning. It was a battle for the most part of my life. Thank God the war is over.

Title #22

In Touch

I am one of GODS children; I am not made of stone
Although at one time, I held hate; to the bone
I had a finger, that pointed at everyone; everywhere
All faults of my brother's, I sure was aware
I would ridicule others, I'd babble on, babble on
I talked through my neck, my heart it was gone
I am only a man; I only looked with my eyes
Now my FATHER reminds me, sometimes you see lies

From Darkness To The Wonderful Light

GOD opened my heart, now I see more clear

Though often it hurts, my eye's sometimes tear

We are told of five senses; our eyes hold just one

Our hearts hold much more, though often it's shun

Try using your heart, though it may take a toll

It truly is special; it's in tune with your soul

Please live through your heart that is how to get home

I hope to see you in heaven, not with the devil to roam

For those with hard hearts I will pray every night

GOD please touch their hearts, give then some insight

Statement of Enlightenment 22

At one time in my life I was not in touch with my heart. I had closed it up to everyone, everything and the idea of there being a God. And it was just fine like that for a long time. I had already mastered the skill of blocking pain in it – it was simple. Just don't use it and it can't get hurt. I am so blessed that I finally was able to put it back in working order. The reason I say this is because along with not feeling pain. You also veto the idea of feeling love, or compassion. And let me tell you, the pain it sometimes feels is well worth the satisfaction I get with love and compassion when I opened up my heart a little it gave God a chance to get in it. I feel that the heart is the doorway to your soul and as it says in the Bible, he will knock, and all you have to do is let him in. And there it is. Once I let the Lord into my heart, everything became much clearer. My eyes did not just see what was in front of me anymore. They also started to see in me. The truth that I thought I saw before was nothing to the real truth that I started to see in myself. I was living, or should I say I was alive, but I surely wasn't living, and almost overnight I was able to stop pointing at others, and realize that when I did, I had three other fingers pointing at myself. And thought it hurts sometimes, I do feel that it keeps me in touch with the Lord.

Title #23

Another day

I'm so tired, I'm so weak

I am down, still I'm crashing

It is my life that I am bashing

I try to keep, my pain within

But I will spread it, once again

You may hurt me, that's not so bad

I mostly hurt myself, it's pretty sad

From Darkness To The Wonderful Light

Please keep your guard up, I will hurt you

I don't think twice, this also true

When your face, is in the sand

I may reach out extend a hand

But again, you just don't know

I may draw back, and strike a blow

I'm somewhat blind, it's hard to see

The actions that will, come from me

Medication helps, to ease the pain

I'm so confused, am I insane?

Because right now it's pretty sad

In a split second, I may go mad

Sometimes I pray, before I sleep

Not to wake,, sometimes i weep

I know I'll wake, on the next day

Then life goes on the same way

Statement of Enlightenment 23

What a familiar feeling. I have found out recently that life can be a beautiful thing. Though there was a time in my life where I did not see this or think it could be possible. Though today I see it as beautiful, it can be hard. The world can beat a man down trials and tribulations are just a part of it. Remember we are not in paradise. And many of us never will be before finding GOD, I saw no light in my life. I felt only the pains of the world and it beating me. And with the beating me so much, I in turn began to fight life myself. Everything of my life seemed like a battle, the sense of peace was not in me. I was tried, tried of the nasty looks, attitudes and the sense of knowing that it would never end. I was always on guard and ready to hurt others, before they hurt me. It seemed the more I thought this way, the more I would end up hurting myself. The word trust was not in my vocabulary I did not trust others, nor did I trust myself. I was definitely wound up tight, and confused. I had also seen many doctors trough the veteran's hospitals and private practices. They all basically said the same thing, that I was a bipolar manic man. There was more drugs; self-medication did not help. It only intensified my already impulsive behaviors. Then there were the drugs they gave me; klouipin, respadol, volume, and a few others. Well they did not help at all. They only turned me into a zombie. And it did intensify frustration. Everything in everybody life became a chore. For so long I had felt like throwing in the towel and calling a quits to my life. Damn, I was tired.

Title #24

Storm Chaser

Through many years in my life, I've gained some control, But to conquer it all, I have not reached that goal. I don't want people to find, that I'm no stranger to pain, but I'm afraid they'll find out, if I snap and go insane. When too many fools are around me and ignorance spews very loud, I may strike out like

From Darkness To The Wonderful Light

lightning, straight from a

storm cloud. Like a storm when it's brewing, even right

till it's end, Be ready for a mess, on this you may

depend. I have seen many of doctors; some say I'm

sick I am ill. Many times I am on edge, so I depend on

a pill. To lose control, I don't like this, I feel my heart

holds knife, I've been destructive forever; I've lived

quite a hard life I don't like life like this, I feel the

sense I am strapped, Shock treatments may help;

maybe I need to be zapped.

Statement of Enlightenment 24

For many years I have been one who solely reacts on impulse. To give anything a second thought was not likely to happen. As a result of living likes this I have been physically hurt many times. It seems that after so long that physical pain was something I had just got used to. To show weakness in the streets is far more deadly than a broken bone or severed artery. And to lay down and give up on any certain encounter could lead to death. So through time I have become very durable. I'm not saying that I am such a devastating force, only that I am or was very stubborn and found' it impossible to quit or give in. being that way it was even hard for me to surrender to GOD. Well dealing with people in the manor that I did, after a while everything and everyone irritated me. Enough was enough, and when I got to that point I would explode in anger. And being one that is not very large in statue; many people thought that they could get over on me or that I was no threat, needless to say I have proven many wrong. And during the after math it most always left me regretting what I had done. For many times I over did it during my act of destruction. I often pleaded with people not to push me, and I would continue for longer than I felt I should have had to. Several times I have even hurt the few people that have been close to me. There physical body often left them nervous to be around me when I was in a sense of anger. All though my children knew not to push an issue; they often were the one ones who could ever calm the storm.

Title #25

Seeds

I've approached many people, planted many of seeds

But the soil from some hearts, nothing grows except

weeds I'm so glad that there's those, that still walk in

GODS light

Their kind words and fellowship, keep my faith day and
Night When I meet those with good hearts, it touches
mine and it grows, it helps me to deal, with lifer lashes
and blows Sometimes I feel like I'll break down, or I

may lash out Back That's the one thing that scares me,
I may go totally whack I've been hurt many times, I'm
excepting of this I fear I might lash out, I may kill; I
won't miss So reach to the LORD, I pray for self-control
I've found a life without JESUS, takes a terrible toll
Some hearts don't know JESUS, many hateful and
mean without the LORD in you, the devil is seen

Statement of Enlightenment 25

Through my times of finding the Lord, I was trying to change my mindset. For me, it didn't happen overnight. Changing my mindset has been an ongoing act, as far as I can remember it wasn't like that with my spirit that seemed to change almost instantly. I was truly trying to walk Christ like very shortly after I had felt I was saved. Shortly after I had felt I was saved. Bad habits were hard to change. It seemed that the more seeds that I was attempting to plant for the lord. The more the devil was pulling them up. I found it difficult in many cases to except people's ugliness when I was trying to be a good person. Smiling and being pleasant did take effort it seemed as though no matter how hard I tried to plant a seed in some, they just wouldn't accept it that is when I learned through the word that sometimes you must wipe your feet and move on. And even dealing with people on a minimum level, I often got ugliness directed at me. It got pretty hard at times, to the point that I was losing faith-in mankind. Today I know that is wrong. Those times when I felt overwhelmed God came through for me. He had always put another Christian in my path for me to fellowship with and it was always very strong and uplifting. GOD is great and he knows just when to lift me up when I am down. I was just like and infant just learning to walk. And GOD has held my hand till I could walk on my own. Today I am starting to run! And now I am armed by GOD and can handle many blows that the devil sends my way. And I am wise enough not to tempt him though.

Title #26

Reach out

Many people have addictions, there compelled to drugs, they drink. They'll say there life is ok, that's what they truly think.

Some know there life is sinking; there in pain they are aware, They know that they have loved ones, it's not important they don't care.

Some have no one at all in life; they give up, there on

their knees. They lose the love for their selves, many
die from this disease

Many minds are lost from an overdose, it's never
realized. Mental wards is where they might end up,
they are institutionalized.
Many addicts go into a jail; they are locked up in a cell.
Withdrawals are a short problem, while they're in a
concrete hell.
Some know that they are drowning - they know there
in quicksand. Some are blessed some that they still
have the sense, to reach out to a helping hand.

Statement of Enlightenment 26

This is a direct reflection of my life at one time. Addiction is a very big problem here in America again, I know firsthand. For many years I was a functional addict. What I mean is that I held a job took care of the family and socialized. After so long I realized that I was no longer functional, that the drugs moved up the ladder in the priority department. My family and what they thought became less important to me as time went on after so much of showing lack of concern for my family, they through it back at me I do not blame them one bit. But I did lose my family where it came to the point where I had no one at all. I was alone. I was on my knees at this point. Then the addiction really kicked in, no longer were drugs for recreational use, they were a necessity to keep the pain of being alone away. I have overdosed many more times than I can remember. I had been so hard on myself that I did institutionalize myself for short periods of time. And I have had many tell me that I was out of my mind, that there had to be something wrong with me. And I do agree, not that I was mentally retarded, but I do know that I was unstable. Jails were inevitable. For drugs, violence, and theft. I did not ever go through physical withdrawals but the mental ones were devastating. I am very blessed! I am one of a very few that still had the sense to reach out to a helping hand. That hand that I reached out to belonged to our lord. I am so thankful that he has always been there, and that I finally realized it.

Title #27

Why Can't You

God works in so many, many people they claim often

forgetting the day, that Jesus was slain,

stones were thrown at our savior, God must have been

crying, I'm sure the devil was pleased, as he saw God's

Son dying.

Jesus spoke to his father, asked to spare all their lives

From Darkness To The Wonderful Light

it is merely the devil, he fills them with lies

Father I know you could save me, but please save

mankind so many can't see, they are lead; they are

blind So if Jesus forgave, the hate in so many others

won't you forgive, your sisters and brothers.

And if forgiving is something, that's a hard thing to do

Remember it hurts, the spirit God has in you

So whatever the case, Please forgive from the heart

Please; do it now, it's time to start

Statement of Enlightenment 27

Can you imagine where you would be if Jesus did not ask the Father to forgive man while he hung from the cross, whipped and given vinegar to quench his thirst instead of water. Well, you wouldn't be. God could have wiped out the earth in its entirety if it were not for Jesus asking for forgiveness of what man was doing to him. And there are so many today that can't forgive another for the cost of a dollar, a cruel word, or a simple, "well so in so said this. People get hatred in themselves for something as stupid as hearsay. I've never seen anything good come out of revenge, or a spiteful act. Holding a grudge hurts those that it is upon and the one holding it. It is a senseless weight that one carries when they cannot find it in their heart to forgive. When you can learn to forgive others, and only then, you can start forgiving yourself. And as we all know that we may never forget. Yeah, that's right. Remembering and forgetting is involuntary your mind eighter remember or it doesn't. But as far as forgiving, now that, you do have control of! It is not through your mind, but through the heart that we can forgive. They say a mind is a terrible thing to waste, well so are the good feelings of your heart. There are far more positive things to work on than to burden yourself with the problems of he said, she said, he did, she did. Just let it go, give someone a break. More important, give yourself a break. Hate, animosity and ill will, are killers, though they may not hurt your flesh, they will do quite a job on your heart and soul. Why not forgive someone, right now!

Title #28

Pandora's Box

Six sides and eight Corners, may be a box straight
from hell I am lucky to be breathing, that I'm alive just
to tell Some claim they've seen death, on the other
side saw a light I to do claim this; it left me in one hell
of a fright I have danced with the devil, with many
drugs put in me face to face with hell's demons; they
are not one to see

From Darkness To The Wonderful Light

They were beating badly, I had felt my body get slain I
know it sounds crazy, but I am totally sane

They had raped me with hatred, through every orifice
and hole they were hurting me badly, and tormenting
my soul The box called Pandora's; it may open for you
please don't taunt the devil, whatever you do
I pray for your soul, that with GOD you will be
You better pray for yourself, it's not demons you see

Statement of Enlightenment 28

Much of this may seem unbelievable but it is true. I have seen things that were not meant for a man to see. And have felt torment that no living being should ever feel. During times of being heavily under the influence of drugs I feel that I being pulled into another dimension, the dimension of hell. Many stories that have been told from a flat line experience have been of seeing a light a since of going to heaven. I have been on the edge of death many, many times. And what I saw was certainly nothing good. What I saw and felt was similar to that of the demons coming out of the ground like in the movie "Ghost". What happened in that movie was child's play compared to what went on in my experience. Through my experience I have been raped, beaten, talked to the dead, and seen parts of hell. I am not saying that I know much, and I certainly do not want to see more. Again I have opened the door way to hell so many times that I cannot count them. Why? I don't know. A strong curiosity and being a fool who always has to push the envelope. Several times I have had people pounce on me and take me to a hospital many of them have been police officers. And several times I have been lead to a mental facility and told that I should commit myself. I thought that was absurd. The only crazy part of the whole thing was the reality that I kept pushing myself to the same devastating limit. What I saw is real; I am not insane for what I saw. Though, I may be for wanting to see it so many times. This is no joke, do not tempt the devil!

Title #29

Fear For You

End of days are real close, I feel that it's near

Many may see hell, it's something I fear

Everywhere that you look, there's the mark of the

beast The devil's took many, he's having a feast

So many don't see they walk around blind

They have no LORD in them, there's so much they

From Darkness To The Wonderful Light

won't find

Some will sell their soul, as a fee for some fame

They don't know the value, it's a terrible shame

Others may kill you, for a few measly dollars

As the devils behind them, as he hoots and he hollers

Others believe their own highest power

I surely believe, that makes the lords stomach sour

Religions corrupt, they twist so much of the truth

some believe they are saved, if they confess in a booth

Hail Mary, Hail Mary, many people they say

To get into heaven, I don't think that's the way

So confess to the LORD, not to a priest

Give the Lord credit, for that much at least

There's only one that you pray to, that's the LORD up

above Give him all of your praise; give him all of your

love So the fear that I have, is not there for me

It's for all that are blind, for all that don't see

Statement of Enlightenment 29

This poem is written from what I see, and from how I feel. Many of you may be offended others may understand my point of view. I did not write this to please anyone or offend; I just hope that it does slap you in the face. I feel the mark of the beast is everywhere, computers, money cards, bar codes, and chips that our government know's everything about everyone. His where abouts are, and his past. The mighty dollar is also something that destroys people. How much is enough? Then there are so many that see the problem in others and not themselves. And try to reach out to the lord. This is good but I must say that I am not one to reach out to the lord through another man. Nor am I one that believes that repetitive prayer is the answer. There is one GOD and only one that you should pray to. I feel that GOD is one that we can speak to, and I do mean speak to through the heart. We are all individuals and all have free will and minds. So I feel that most prayers should be a personal experience. Not a prayer that is heard by the lord by quotes. Any person with half a brain can repeat what they have heard, or read. So many of us walk around blind without an insight of the plain truth. The truth only GOD gave his only son so that we could be forgiven of our sins. And through JESUS(only). We may make it to heaven we are not a high power and there is only one who is and I feel that is not as complicated as many wish it to be. I believe it is as simple as repenting to the lord and simply asking for forgiveness. Though it must be done with the upmost sincerity and directly from an open heart. So please stop looking at a statue, close your eyes and speak to GOD.

PLEASE!!

Title #30

Northwest

I am here at Northwest

There are many around

Some people depressed – most there

Life they have frowned

Then here there are others – who are mentally

impaired. Some they see demons – there

Whole life they are scared

Then there are those – dependent on drugs

From Darkness To The Wonderful Light

The desire makes no difference – cause

Here you get hugs

We all get a chance – to ease the stress in our mind

Most the staff helps – they understand

They are kind

Know one did know – But I should have been dead.

But the doors here at Northwest – I walk through

instead My destruction hurts me – I get violent and

burst I am so glad to be here – instead of a hurst

I Know that at times – I go a little insane

That's ok with me – I feel this place share my pain

Facts are I walked in here a Broken down man

If I foresaw the care they give – I sure would have ran

Statement of Enlightenment 30

I had written this poem during a time of darkness. Just like so many times before I had complicated my life to the point where I was heavily burdened with homicide and suicidal thoughts. I had run myself to the ground by pushing the envelope to the point of near death. I defiantly needed a break so I felt that checking myself into an institution for a little self-control and a reality check. Northwest is the name of a rehab hospital that resides in San Antonio Texas. I was the poster child for a broken down man when I walked through the doors. The place was great; I felt that it was exactly what I needed at the time. What really made the biggest impact were the other residents. What I saw were people that defiantly had major problems. Although every person there had different issues, not one person's problem was more devastating than the next. I don't know if it was intentional that every person faced different issues, but it sure did help me to not think of my own problems. We all heard difference stories while in group sessions, and were able to reflect on them. Many times I found it hard to reach up to a hand in order to get help. At this place there were so many caring hands that were right next to me. I was surrounded by misfits, and I do not exclude myself together, we all helped each other to gain some strength. And when I think of the staff there, well they showed genuine concern and care. What I found out, is that most of the staff had under gone certain trails, and tribulations in their own past, that is one major asset that intrigued me. I have been through the system many times and most of the time I was treated like a broken machine that was going through an assembly line. Whatever the situation, just take these pills and come back in a couple weeks for a progress report. What fools you, run into who hold degrees, people are all different, and should be treated as such.

Title #31

Who's The Fool?

This child that I met – pushed from one place to
another I think that he's also pushed away from his
Mother This boy every day – He reached out for
attention To irritate all others – was not his intention
I've been in a group with him – for a short while.
When I am around him – he gives me a smile
To others around – he's a thorn in their side
Most people feel this – it's something they hide

I see many people here – push him away

Some People they do this – in the most hateful way

In a very short time – in this place he won't be

He's asking so many – "will you miss me"

This woman he just asked "am I one that you'll miss"

"No, I won't miss you" yeah, she answered like this

The way that It came out – to me it was sick

When I heard this response, my hatred came quick

I hope that she's clueless – about sounding so cold

And not by intention – to be hateful and bold

To me the response – it was not very cool

As intelligent as she is – she sure is the fool

Statement of Enlightenment 31

Once again I was in a rehab slash mental ward. A place where I fit in very well. I don't quite remember what facility that I was in, but I do remember the situation between a staff member and a patient, Damn, I remember those feeling of wanting to strike out at someone to the point I had to isolate myself. I did manage to regroup my thoughts for a minute, and that's when I sat down and wrote this poem. The situation involved a mentally retarded boy who was 18 years old, but had the mind of a 7 year old. So what I saw, was a little boy who was surrounded by strangers who had been thrown away by his family. I do remember that the facility did not have the means to care for somebody with his needs. And what I found out was that they were only able to provide limited help for a limited time due to legal issues. Anyway this (little Boy) often could get a little over bearing and obnoxious, but what child doesn't at one time or another. I remember he was scared, he was always asking people, and I mean everyone (Do you love me?) in the most innocent way. This little boy starved for affection, who could blame him. This was the situation. The day before he knew he was leaving, he would go around asking people (are you gonna miss me). Well when he asked one of nurses this question, she replied in the most hateful way (No! I won't miss you.) When I saw the boy's face, it looked as if his whole world crumbled. I felt instant rage. Although I never hurt women, children, old people, or those who are not in their right mind. I did picture myself strangling her. I know that's wrong and I wouldn't physically hurt any women. So, I tried to put my feelings on paper. In my eyes it was the nurse that was the fool, not the mentally handicapped boy.

Title #32

Dead Weight

I've fed this flesh for 35 years – A little bit more
It's feasted on all – that comes from hells core
It never goes hungry – I feed it so much
The flesh that I have – it's in Satan's clutch
Anything good – the flesh banishes it fast
Not a thing that is scared – ever does last
I'm so use to destruction – I start destroying myself
I must take all the evil – and put it high on a shelf
If I hadn't a spirit – I would live in shear bliss
Cause whatever was good – I sure wouldn't miss

But that's not the case – I have a spirit that's strong
It yearns for God's love – it knows right from wrong
When I reflect on myself – past the flesh I must look

If I didn't do that – my own life I would have took
So I know of my spirit – it walks in Gods light
It's in war with my flesh – every day every night
So this spirit I have – carries one hell of a load
It carries this flesh – down this long narrow road
I'm grateful for one thing – this flesh's getting old.
Soon it will be – in the ground bought and sold
Then I will be – right where I want to be
that's walking in heaven – with the Lord next to me

Statement of Enlightenment 32

I don't really know exactly when this poem was written. But I do know that it is about many years of my life, even when I was in dark and living very sinful, I was in fact aware of the good in me that wanted to shine. I still don't understand why it is that for so many years I was drawn to evil ways. I guess it's because such a pretty picture was painted by Satan. I fed my flesh in abundance – sex, drugs, money and power. There was nothing that I would not do or anyone that I would let get in my way of these things. Hurting people physically, financially or mentally was never a problem, until the act was done, because after the flesh got its fill, I then would reflect and feel remorse. I know it sounds stupid, but that's how it was for many years. Then later on in life I started to think a little before I acted. I started thinking about the pain my heart would go through after feeding the flesh. Damn! I felt as though I was being torn apart. I have only for the past few years, begun to feed the spirit more than the flesh, and the more I feed the spirit, the easier it is to keep reins on the flesh. And today I do realize that half or maybe more of my life has been living for Satan, and that is very wrong. I've lived very selfish, just worried about what would bring me instant gratification. Today I am living quite differently. It took some effect, but I have found out that being selfless can be very rewarding, and I can finally look in the mirror and be pleased in who I see. Today is beautiful, and I'm so blessed that I am a new me. I am no longer like the tin man.

Title #33

Lady By The Bus

Early one morning, I met a lady – she was hurt, she was crying. Her husband of many years - beat her down, Left her lying

From a truck that was moving, she got pushed out in the road. To me there's no excuse, to get in that mode

She was wrapped up in bandages, she looked pretty bad She held no ill feelings, but she certainly was sad

From Darkness To The Wonderful Light

I asked her "dear lady what can I do? She said, "Yes",
May I please have a hug there from you

As we hugged, we both felt the Lord, at the same time
We both asked for forgiveness, for the man's hate and
his crime.

There were blessings that day, at least three that I
know of To both of us and that man, from the Lord up
above I myself feel, I am blessed, more than most
By the father, the Son, and Holy Ghost

Statement of Enlightenment 33

This was written during a time in my life when I was going through some serious soul searching. I don't quite remember what state I was in at the time, due to the fact that I was roaming around the U.S. for some time. I remember I was at a greyhound station early in the morning when I noticed this lady crying off in a corner at the bus station. I immediately had to find out if there was any way I could help her. And that's when she simply asked me for a hug. We had started talking about all the evil things people do, and wondered what compels people to do such. We had both discussed of the tribulations that we were going through, and came to the conclusion that we were still blessed. We both felt that we were blessed because neither one of us had ill feelings against anyone that we could think of. We then had a little prayer to GOD, along with praise for keeping our hearts soft. And to my amazement she then prayed for the man who had treated her like he did. Wow! It makes me think of what a beautiful man Jesus must have been. And I am referring to the time when he was on the cross down Calvary Road. Just to think of how Jesus asked GOD to forgive us, when we were crucifying him. And knowing that without His asking GOD to forgive us, man may have been wiped off the earth. Wow Again! I feel and again, this is just my way of thinking. But when you extend out your heart to another, Both are blessed, the giver and receiver though the man who did wrong had no idea that he was being prayed for, we knew and GOD the same and when I say that I feel that I am blessed more than most, I do believe it. GOD constantly puts stuff in front of me that feeds my spirit, just when it needs it. No matter what I am going through. He always shows me that there are others to think about, and how so many have hard hearts and walk in darkness. Yes! GOD is Great.

Title #34

Mine

It makes my day, if it makes your day, if you
puzzled with the life that I live
I've been dealt certain cards from the Lord up above,
it is something he gave, nothing you give
If my life it seems shocking or somewhat care free
Just realize you're you, and I will always be me
Were you neglected or beaten in those years as a child
or did a silver spoon feed you, was your life kind of

From Darkness To The Wonderful Light

mild Did you ever go hungry, was love given or nill

do you have a big hole, desperately trying to fill?

Are there those with arms open? Loved for whatever

you are or thrown away by so many, does your heart

have a scar

odd I may be, I may walk through life strange

through your eyes there may be, so much to arrange

I do the best that I can, try to smile each day

I except what God gives me, I know no other way

Life sometimes gets rough; it's put me down on my

knees But I'm blessed every moment, though it's not

what one sees

and I will never give up, I will always move on, till

the day I am buried, and my last breath is gone

Until that day comes, every day a new hat

I will change it quite often to suit where I'm at

I'll live hard to work and work hard to live

I don't look for handouts or expect most to give

My flesh may be beaten; I walk hard and also meek

But my spirit is strong; you won't find one part that's
weak sometimes making bad choices, but they are
ones that I choose in every choice I gain something,
and there's something I lose
All I can say, is that this here life it is mine
What's really important is with the Lord I am fine

Statement of Enlightenment 34

I have noticed through my fifty years of life that too many people are looking at others when they should try taking a look at themselves. It hurts me to say; But my Father's expectations and disappoints in me were often hard to deal with, and that's only because I love him so much. Though he is and was such a great man in my eyes, he is still (Him). And we may be so different in many ways, I except him for whatever he is and all of his ways. And I have come to the conclusion, that I, and I alone must accept who I am and all my ways. So, now being able to except (Me). I then can accept others, without trying to change them to suit myself. And now that I am a parent, I have vowed to love and accept my own children for whatever they do, or are. Though they may hurt me or just right out piss me off at times, that's ok, I except them unconditionally, and I will never denied them and I do realize that a huge percentage of the people involved directly in my life have pointed fingers at me and couldn't understand my thoughts' or actions for the life of them. And I also realized that many disappointments were due to the fact that many couldn't deal with what they saw as self-destruction in myself. And many of them just down right gave up, and wiped their feet of me. Well if you love someone, you don't do that! I feel that we are all this earth just as GOD wants or allows us to be, from the Holy to the unholy. The robbers and the givers. The clean and unclean. When a person sees another who is bad in every way that you can think of, pray for that man and if possible help them. If you can't find it in your heart to think this way, (I hope someone prays for you.) Maybe just maybe, GOD has these people around for the intent to reach others. And though I have been down on my knees, ate off the ground, and slept in the dirt. I have done much of this to myself. But guess what? I'm happy with who I am, and I know GOD is also. So, if you want to go around pointing at others. Have at it, maybe one day you'll get your fill.

Title #35

CHARACTER

Trust goes a long way, in whatever you do. If you cannot be trusted, people won't look at you.

A man with good character, He is trustworthy you bet. He is one that most people are glad they have met.

If you work for a man, give it all that you got. You surely won't be a man that is forgot.

Like a dime to a dozen, you will find some that slack. If you are one that's like this, you may leave not come back. Work for what you get, it's the best way to live. Don't wait for handouts or someone to give.
God gave you something, that your life here on earth, he is always one giving, from the day of your birth.
When your noticed do you want to be looked at sideways. If not keep good character all of your days.

And remember thank God, that you are here, that you live. You can show thanks not taking through your life try to give.

Statement of Enlightenment 35

I remember the days before I had GOD in my life. I had character, and plenty of it. The problem was, that it was bad character. So many did not want to be around me, many doors were slammed in my face. Though many I have kicked open! Which didn't help, it was like a contagious plaque, that everything that I touched turned to shit. People wanted something dirty done, a deed, I was the one. How bad! And what a dirty taste it left in my mouth. I feel that there are two ways that you can lean toward. The good being of GOD, and the bad, being of the devil, Oh! Character you will have no matter which side you are leaning toward. But the good goes with good, and the bad goes with bad. And when you are one of bad character, it's really not important what other's think cause at least in my time, I didn't care about myself. And to change your character from bad to good isn't always that easy. It takes time, especially when you're trying so hard to change and all you get is those ill feelings directed at you. People will get there ideas of you and will stick with those ideas. For a while; Hell! My own Father is one like this. He knows Peter James Martinez, the one who robs, steals, thinks about himself, and is just no good. But guess what? I will not and haven't let me stop from changing for the better. Many may never accept you. But the important one is. Do you except yourself. When you don't give up, GOD won't give up. And I must tell you, it is a lot better today seeing welcome mats at the doors instead of go away, there's nobody here. Don't let others rain on your parade!

Things, if you work at it, will get better. Have faith, and if you lack faith pray for it. I know it's helped me. I am no longer a taker. Today and from now on I will be a giver – redemption is worthwhile.

Title #36

DOOMED

Just got back from the nurse – she just gave me a pill.

It helped ease anxiety – Around these mentally ill.

The sergeant, those who – moved me to a new block.

They understand my dilemma – to my amazement my shock.

The first man I met – said he sent a man straight to

hell. I'm sure they'll cross paths – He just as well.

Then right next to me – a man has one leg that's lame.

135

From Darkness To The Wonderful Light

The man that ran him over didn't stop – what ashamed

The man next to him – has it worst most of all.

Disease, ignorance and darkness – before the Lord he

may fall.

Further on down there's a boy there – He's crying.

I only speculate this – without mom he is dying

Another flamboyant – holds the demon of greed. And

he kisses ass like a slave – never be freed, only ten

days ago my world it was vast – it went pretty far

today. I have four walls – and bars, it went pretty fast

Behind a steel bar, and I also have found – that your

world no matter what size.

That when you take a good look – few are blessed in

my eyes.

Statement of Enlightenment 36

A time of despair, loneliness, rage, and walking in darkness. I had and could foresee no chance of my life getting better. I had felt abandon by all, even the Lord. And to make it worse I was on medication for bipolar disorder, which often resulted in rage. Of course the heavy cocaine addiction didn't help. Jail was just part of life, in and out on a regular basis. The reason I was incarcerated during this time, I am clueless about. I do remember being put in a cell with 23 other inmates in my block. And I also remember snapping. I also remember getting shackled, gagged an throw in a rubber padded room. After a few hours I was able to focus and calm down. The problem was this. When they processed me in, they put me in a block with young wanna be little gangsters. Damn, they were irritating. The nest thing I remember was getting in a physical confrontation. Then I blacked out in a rage. Not to long after the incident, a nurse had medicated me and advised the sergeants that I needed to be in the psych ward, or block. I had defiantly agreed. That's when I wrote this poem. Writing always seemed to calm me down, and I felt more comfortable with those who dealt with mental issues. Yeah! Sounds strange, but true. Through most psychotics are unpredictable. I find that they also allow more space. Due to the fact they or we, or I need it. So with the understanding that if ones space is invaded, that it will likely stir up chaos, space is given. And believe it or not I found being locked up in that block very relaxing. A lot, more than my life outside the bars was. As far as blessings go, I saw none in or out of jail. Except maybe the blessing of being locked up for a while. Life seemed like hell. Jail was my sanctuary many of times.

Title #37

REACH OUT

Many people have addictions – there compelled to

drugs, they drink, they'll say there life is OK – that's

What they truly think.

Some know their life is sinking – there in pain they are

aware. They know that they have loved ones – it's not

important they don't care.

From Darkness To The Wonderful Light

Some have no one at all in life – they give up, there on

their knees they lose the love for themselves. Many die

from this desire.

Many minds are lost from an overdose - it's never

realized mental wards are where they might end up –

they are institutionalized.

Many addicts go into a jail – they are locked up in a

cell, withdraws are a short problem – while there in a

concrete hell. Some know that they are drowning –

they know they're in quick sand, they are blessed that

they still have the sense to reach out to a helping

hand.

Statement of Enlightenment 37

When I say many, I do mean that there are or a least must be. Could I be the only one battling addiction. Though I am talking about myself in this poem. I see the problem everywhere. Be it alcohol, drugs, food, money, sex, power, more, more, more, more, more, I have been a glutton to all. Every since I was a young child, I remember being one to push the envelope. I would eat cookies till I vomited, drank milk till it came out my nose. And also I went through my share of physical pain. Everything had to be faster; I had to go higher, the more dangerous, the more fun. Though it is a problem for many children, it is one that is often overlooked. Due to the fact that most, not all have peers or elders that pull back on the reins so to speak. So many children learn that there is a limit. Then there are those like myself. No limits, no boundaries, go ahead see what happens. I have found out that the more you feed any addiction. The stronger it gets, it can and it has for me, gotten stronger than the love for myself, for others and even the Lord. And after this happened, I surrendered to my addictions. I binged and purged, drank till I blacked out. And did cocaine to many near death experiences. It didn't stop there. Soon I found myself getting addicted to the near death experience. WOW! After years of this and going in and out of jails, along with being in mental institutions. I came to the realization, that what I had heard my whole life about there not being anything wrong with me. I found that to be wrong itself. There was something wrong and there always has been and will be. But to tell that to those that only see Black and White is a waste of time. For a blind man, never will know what it's like to see! And also through my experiences. I have found that almost all will give up on you. If you are one who knows what I mean, than you also know that to give up on, yourself follows close behind others. I had went along with those and gave up on myself also. But I am and was blessed, GOD did not give up on me and he also communicated with me. You may think I'm crazy, But that's ok. I've been called worse. Through these near death experiences, the Lord allowed me to see things. Things that we as living breathing people don't see. He has let me see glimpses of hell. I have fought demons, spoke to the spirits of those that love me, while letting me hear them after I had died. The pain and anguish that I have put many through, the falling of others, due to my death wish. I have spoken to others, only to have another spirit take over in order to speak to me. I know that a lot of you, right now are probably saying. "Yeah, he still should be in a mental hospital." But that's ok too. I didn't write this for you. I wrote this for those that have or are at this moment destroying their lives for those that feel that they are crazy, for those that GOD is trying to reach, and if this is you, try GOD, reach out to his helping hand. P.S. Don't let go.

Title #38

Rise & Fall

I just spoke to a doctor – I had spoken from the heart. When I take a deep look inside – It starts tearing me apart. I lack some strength in many ways – although I am not weak. I also know I have two faces – I'm aggressive and I'm meek. When others get too close to me – I often make a stand. I am ready to strike out a blow – with a vengeful hand. Children put me at an ease – and women just the

same. My defense – my guard it's put down I am meek
and I am tame. I have fought for many years – I've
fought to live, I've fought for life. To being shot I am
no stranger – or to be stabbed with a knife. This life to
me seems like a game – one that I'm
forced to play, and if my defense is not good enough –
A grave is where I'll lay.
When life is something you may lose – Then this game
is not a game. I have to have a strong offense – I must
make others lame. When I win, surpass them all. I'm
the one on top – and then I fall.

Statement of Enlightenment 38

I remember when I wrote this, what was on my mind was (King of the Mountain). This was a game I used to play as a child. A very rough game. There would be anywhere from six to twelve kids at the bottom of a hill, and the object was to get on the top. No holds barred no protection, and no rules. Well! It seems as if though this game I used to play never ended. The difference now is that the stakes are higher in every way. When trying to make it to the top today, many get hurt or end up dead. I am generally a soft spoken person who also walks softly. But I have been playing a game in which I feel I must be the king of the mountain. By achieving this goal I have devastated many, along with destroying others. Not being one who enjoys seeing others beaten down it has often got overwhelming. I had felt while destroying others, the sense of self destruction. When it gets to this point I often found myself talking to doctors in order to relief the inner pain that I would endure. Physically I can handle more than the average person. But emotionally not so. I have walked around with a very strong defense and offense at the same time. But sometimes it is in order for a break, or to quit playing. Not so easy! Sometimes you get pulled back into it, even if you don't want it. And it seems that whenever I get the sense and feeling that I'm on top. It never fails, I fall right back down to the bottom where I have to start over again. Today I have decided that I will not participate in trying to be king of anything. From the stands as a spectator, I get a better view and it's not as dangerous. And now I can see from a different angle. If your soul goal is to be above everyone else, you're a fool, playing a fool's game.

Title #39

Cherish

Love and cherish your life, because it will not last.

Death will come quickly, and it will come fast.

The choices while living, will determine your fate.

Do you live with love, or live life with hate.

Were you kind to your brothers or sisters the same.

If you end up in darkness you have no-one to blame.

So worship the Lord, keep love in your heart.

Do not let the devil, tear your life apart, cause if you

Walk in his shadow, live life with his SIN. Your chances for heaven, they will grow thin. So repent all your sins, thank the Lord that you live. If you do this its paradise, that the Lord will surely give. The narrow path we should walk, sometimes hard to abide. The flesh it is sinful, the Lord knows of our hide. The devil will tempt and taut you, most all of the day. He is working against God, in the most awful way. Just try to walking Christ-like, the best that you can. And know there are angels around you, since your life began.

Statement of Enlightenment 39

When I say cherish your life that includes everyone involved in it. From your family to your foes and those you love or despise. I have been one in the not so long ago past, who simply cherished nothing, and it has brought regret. My Mother being a big reflection of not cherishing another which held some kind of parallel effect on my own life in a very hurtful way. I had gone for several years without communicating with her, due to lack of appreciation and concern. I had taken her for granted as I did many more things in my life. I did not cherish the moments that we spent together, or the times we were apart. And then one day I got a phone call! Tragedy! Well, today I do not have that satisfaction of saying; "We spent many wonderful times together." What does go through my head is; "Damn! I never took the time to show her how much I loved her. "So in fact, not cherishing the ones you love, just one day may bite you in your own ass. And just as loved ones, I have found it important to cherish those that you may hold resentment toward. I say this from experience. While I lived in Niles, Michigan as an Ironworker. I had a friend that was always around to help me drink beer, and get high well I remember one day we were at another house drinking, when for whatever reason, he smacked me upside the head. Instant rage over took my mindset, but I held back. Shortly afterward I gave him a ride back to his house, only after driving down a dirt road in the country. I cracked his jaw and gave him two broken ribs, my mindset was (he brought it upon himself).Every time that man saw me after that he would run the other way. He was terrified. One month later that man froze to death in his own backyard. And now today I look back at how I made this man's last few days on earth. I did not cherish his life, friendship, or his family's or loved ones. Over putting my ignorant pride above all. Today I try, with a passion to cherish all in life, you know what? Nothing last forever here on Earth. In the blink of an eye GOD may call upon someone that is a part of your life. Or he may very well call on you. The reasons that GOD, calls upon us is something that I will not even for a second try to figure out. But being one to be blessed enough to get a glimpse of what darkness and evil can await some. I surely have come to my senses to not tempt. I have a strong belief that living in hate and sin will only bring eternal suffering. If GOD can cast his most beautiful angel out of heaven, just my guess. That he may do the same to all of that angels followers, and please remember that if you think your life is a long going process, how do you compare it to eternity.

Title #40

Agape

Agape love is something, a love that's not perceived.

God had this love for all of us, before we were

conceived. He gave us free will and a road; he hopes

that we will follow.

When temptations guide us off this road, I know it

brings him sorrow.

From Darkness To The Wonderful Light

With the free will that he gave, think of your choices well because if were making bad ones, we could end up in hell, The Lord wants us in heaven; hold out your arms to him, If you do not do this, your new life could be grim. He wants us all in heaven, to walk right by his side. So he gave us all a Bible, on which we should abide. I'd like to see all people that are upon this earth. To see the gates of heaven, upon there great rebirth. To all my brothers and sisters, I'll pray for you and me. I hope that when in heaven, it's you that I will see.

Statement of Enlightenment 40

From my understanding, Agape love is a love that is so strong and precious that only GOD is able to hold it. WOW! My mind can't even imagine how much strength that kind of love could hold. As far as we go, when we love someone we want them to love us back, and in some way show it. I know, to this day how it feels not to get it back, and in some way show it. I know to this day how it feels not to get it back when you give it. It kinda stings! But, we do move on, because there is little or nothing we can do to change it. But I also know the wonderful feeling you get when you receive love back. I get this from my children. I can't imagine the toll it would take on me if I thought for one minute they didn't love me. I know we have angered and disappointed each other a few times, but that's life, and through love, many things can be over looked and thrown out. For all these reasons, I believe it's the sole intent of having free will. I don't believe that GOD wants anything more than for us to choose to love him. Wants us to hold our arms out to him, and show him through our acts how much we love him. He even left us a guide. I know it makes me feel good when my children tell me and show me that they love me. So, let's make Father GOD feel good, because we want to.

Title #41

Circles

I am running in circles – all places I'm lost.

Self-destructions an impulse – at a very high cost.

Skills, knowledge and wisdom – are but a few that
I hold.

I'm so blessed, so gifted – by many I'm told.

I easily obtain just about anything I yearn.

I can conquer a mountain – but what do I learn.

The sad truth about this – is my life's no way to live

From Darkness To The Wonderful Light

I destroy all that is good – I guess I'm just like a sive.

Overdosing on drugs – many times it's not new,

It's like Russian roulette – that's my life, I am true,

I've been in hell a few times – demons have tortured

me, The Lord is a Good one – for his forgiveness I plea,

I will bend over backwards – to help all fellow men.

I've put others above me – many times and again

There is something that's missing – there's some kind

of hole. It may be in my mind – at least not in my soul.

I've had many possessions, to me there just things.

Maybe I'll get contentment – when the fat lady sings.

Statement of Enlightenment 41

Nothing sacred, nothing holy! Oh a time I remember so well, and am so blessed to be able to share it, and be alive. A time when I was not aware of GOD's awareness. Knowing that GOD loved me and had a purpose for me was not in my mindset. What my mind did say is "no-one cares, loves or thinks about you in any good way!" And do ya know who that no-one was? It was me, I didn't understand it, and to be truthful I still don't. I've always cared and loved others more than myself, which doesn't say a whole lot, considering that I had none for myself. But never the less, I would rather starve to death before I would let a few others die of starvation. I guess what I mean is I don't understand how I could be so selfish and selfless at the same time. Facts are! For a long time I was running around in circles like a chicken with his head cut off, a kid in a candy store. I could go on with the little sayings, but you get the picture. I was out of control. I felt as though, there was nothing that was good in my life. And I didn't have the most important thing (GOD)! So, this being the case, anything that looked, smelled, tasted or felt good, I wanted. And I wanted all of it, and more. The cost or consequences were not important. My life being one of the cost, and on many occasions, there was no thinking things through. Nobody cared what would happen to me, and I surely know I didn't. So what the hell! Let's put a bullet in the chamber, see what happens, for you who have no clue what would drive someone to be this way, consider yourself blessed. And for those that do, please talk to GOD.

He loves you, and guess what? So do I, and I haven't even met you. I have no way of knowing if this means anything to you. But I do hope it can help you to love yourself. I have found that without loving yourself, it's hard to love others. I say this because when you hurt yourself, it does hurt others. Believe it! PS. A couple tears hit this page while writing it.

Title #42

Ignorance

Mom and dad – damn – they influence us all.

By the words that they say – we may rise we may fall.

My father so smart – such a very wise man.

His words hurt me dearly – sometimes I have ran.

His expectations for me – his standards were high.

He doesn't realize – I am me not that guy.

For many of years – I felt disappointment from him.

His blaspheming me – He was clueless of this sin.

He loves me a great deal – he loves me so much.

He's ignorant of the fact – He was my one crutch.

The world is a circus – Satan is the one in charge of this place. Every day in this life – He'll slap you in the face. Realizes mom loves you, and dad just the same.

They really do love you, from those two you came.

So take what is good, ignore what is bad.

Because if I don't – you'll always be sad.

Statement of Enlightenment 42

Ignorance, sounds a little harsh. I could have said "Clueless" but that really doesn't matter. Children will walk their own path, in their own way! No matter what. Little sayings such as half assed, quitter, you could do better, what's wrong with you, are just a few of many such discouraging words. Though they may be little to us as parents, in a child's mind they are strong, and sure we say these things only because we want our children to succeed, and do well in life. And I'm sure some are saying "bullshit"! It may be so. But from my own experience as a child and parent. I have come to believe a few different reactions may erupt! A parent can push and push. But in doing so you run the risk of breaking spirits, getting pushed back, or despise. I was one who had fallen into the broken spirit category. I got that "never say you can't" Thrown at me so much that I had found it easier to never try. And as much as I love my Father, I figured why upset him with the possibility of disappointing him. That went with sports, or any group activities that I could be involved in. The feeling of not meeting up to standards only seemed worse when I was being compared to others. That even went along with family, it seemed as though was compared to them as well. It seemed as if the devil himself was slapping me in the face daily. I know now, as a parent that we all want the best for our children. And I'm sure that I have said and done things out of ignorance that may have a negative effect on them. But the fact is what negative results come from me, were solely unintentional, I try to be supportive, encouraging, and excepting of what they do and who they are. I do try to guide them in a good direction, and I will not push them. They may push back, and what I do want is to keep them close.

Title #43

Killing Your Baby

This woman I saw getting high – while she's pregnant

It's hard to believe she's – so incredible ignorant.

As far as destroying herself – there's not much I can

do. For you future Mother – you're not just hurting

you. It may be a fetus – but it's also a child.

Pay attention to these words – don't take them so

mild. Everyone deserves a fair chance, in life just to

live If you're pregnant and using – do you think this

you give. And if continue to do this – and don't feel

some shame. Think of your baby – being born

somewhat lame.

Statement of Enlightenment 43

Who am I to judge? No-one, that's GOD's job not mine. But I do feel that it is my job to plant a seed for the Lord in order to help stop an individual from hurting one of GOD's children. Especially the weak, innocent and defenseless. We all have our faults, and we must deal with them. And those faults will then be dealt with by GOD; a child is a gift, a blessing, a creation of the Lord. And if you are an expecting Mother who is using ANYTHING that can harm your baby. You should be ashamed. Life can be rough, this world can be cruel. This being, the devils domain, and heaven bring GOD's. Realize that your baby will have to endure all the trails and tribulations that are here on earth before having the chance to see paradise. The devil works 24/7 he does not rest, he is here to seek and destroy. He also has many followers. Those that are cruel and will hurt all those in their path. How unfair can you be if you are the first to bring harm unto your unborn baby. If the world beats your unborn baby. If the world beats your child down because maybe its not as smart, a little slower, weaker, or lame in some way. I hope you realize that you are the one who threw them into shark infested waters, only after you cut them. Say you are going through some sort of ordeal, pain, or just miserable. DEAL with it! Do not pass it on to your child. If you can't handle it, try giving it to GOD. Then maybe he can give you the will, strength, sense and care to think of your child. And think about this, if that baby grows up deformed or sick, they will still probably love you. Now, if someone can love you that much, can't you show enough, not to hurt them.

Title #44

Think About It

Sometimes I feel that I'm alone, and often in despair.

Sometimes in hinders all my faith, sometimes I just

don't care. When these times come I pray real hard,

While looking in the sky. I must remember God is

close; He lives in you and I.

When prayers are not answered, or I think that there

not there. I'll ask the Lord, increase my faith, I'll ask

him in my prayer. Then remembering I am loved, he

gave his son for me. I don't know why this I forget,

because it's plain to see.

He's carried me through the hard times, and walked

right by my side.

I know those times when I've been hurt, we both sat

down and cried.

So next time that I feel despair, I must remember this

That on his own time, he'll call me

The new life will be bliss.

Statement of Enlightenment 44

Throughout my life, often times I do get down and feel a sense of despair I am quite sure that I am not alone. At least I hope not. And sometimes the cause cannot be pin pointed, it may be due to a rain filled day, the devil, or maybe a bipolar cycle. Whatever the reason, I must remember that it will pass. Life does get hard at times and when it does I often pray. Pray for GOD to shed more light my way. And when that light doesn't hit me like a deer in the Ray of a headlight, I pray for faith. At least to strengthen it, and then I remember how much I love my own children, and how it hurts me when I see them not happy or hurt. I remember a time when my daughter had a tear gland tore in her eye. Damn! The pain I had gotten from that would have been a lot less if I could have traded places with her. I'm a strong believer that GOD feels the same with all of his children (you and I). And just as Jesus life was given for us. I would do for my children. So, I keep the faith that soon enough I will be with my true father, (GOD) and life (eternal life) will be great.

Title #45

Were Pigs

From the day we are born – we are glutens from birth.

Most all live life like this – until we leave earth,

When we are babies – we'll drink milk till we burst.

And as we grow older – one beer can't quench our

thirst. There's a biblical story – I'm not sure which one.

A boy made no profit – so this man banished his son,

When we gain a position – we want to move higher,

If you're one who denies this – I think you're a liar,

If payment for something – is only a dollar.

You know you'll want more – you may scream or

holler. Sex, drugs and money – Let's talk of this now,

When it comes to these 3 things – I am a sow

A man wants two women – most men think this way,

Some they want to men – that is if there gay

As a man wants his sugar – till teeth rot out of their

mouth. We are fat lazy creatures – most asses go

south, Some shit here sounds funny – I know this is

true. I have selfish demons – I'll bet you have some to,

Lord please have mercy – we are glutens, we're pigs,

But it started with Adam and Eve in there figs.

Statement of Enlightenment 45

From the President to the wine-o at the park. More power, more votes, more courage, and recognition to the drunk who wants more wine even if he can't stand, more more, more! I know that I am surely one who lived very selfishly in the past. There are only a very few that I can think of that show selfless acts. But the only one that sticks out is when Ron Howard played the part of Opie on the Andy Griffith Show. He conned nickels out of everyone in order to get a coat for a little girl that needed one. But that was only television! The one and only true selfless act was that on Calvary Road, and it may very well stay that way. I do know one thing for sure! I was born with this flesh, just as I was born with a sinful and lustful nature. But, what really important for me today? Is that I try to control it. And the more I have GOD in my life, the easier it gets. Right now in my life I have a duffel bag, it holds everything that I own in this world. I work offshore as a helper with low pay. But guess what? I'm satisfied with everything in my life, have you ever asked the question! "When is enough, enough?" Well there my friends?" Only you have that answer. My answer came to me through GOD. I know he and my children love me. Along with food, water and clothes, what else do I need to be able to smile when I wake up? Sure now that I'm working again, I'll get things. But I will keep it in mind that they are just that, (things). Some of the things I get will be for pleasure and fun, but what I'm really working for is to help my children through school if they want. And to get a big enough place to be able to feed, clothe, and shelter who ever needs my help. I often talk to the Lord of this. I guess when he thinks I can handle it, it will happen. Have you ever heard that saying about the "gift of giving" Well; I find that to be true in a big way today.

Title #46

Mr. Know It All

Like so many in life, you like to talk – not much listen. Consequences not thought of – there's a lot that you're missing. You may toot your own horn – on how you're life it is going. But to spread all of your ways – it is ignorance flowing. I will walk in my shoes – then put my feet in yours next. But until I do this – my opinions will rest. There is no-one alike – no two minds are the same. So when you're thinking for others – you sound a little insane. It may work for you – to show women disgrace. But teach this to another – he may get shot in the face. You may have a good talk – so please watch what you say.

You're like the pied piper – some will follow your way. Through life you're jumped hurdles – you jump them with ease. But for a young man still wet – he may fall to his knees. Remember the young man – that you used to be. Your own way and time – when you stood up to pee. I know you don't mean harm – your intensions are good. Just remember my young man – I was once where you stood.

Statement of Enlightenment 46

Oh, what a fool it is that knows everything. I wrote this while in the valley in Texas. This was due to doing something else that ended me up in accommodations that the state provides. I had gotten into a fender bender along with having no insurance or license. Got me a room in one of the fine jails in Texas. Any ways, while in jail you run into quite an array of people. I particularly remember one man who spewed his ignorance to those that were in need of a role model. There were at least a dozen out of thirty young men under the age of twenty that were in the same cell that I was staying in. As most people know at that age we are still somewhat like a sponge. The problem is that at the age we don't realize what we should gather and what we shouldn't, impressionable we are. What really grabbed my attention is the way one individual had all the young men memorized with his thoughts that made him top inmate. On the how to's and not to's in dealing that made him a leader in the I'm the big dog on campus. He spoke to the young men on the subject of how to dominate, manipulate, and overthrown all those that were part of his life. I did manage to pull the man to the side in order to talk to him a little. And to my amazement he listened a little. I simply asked him if he would want his boy or child to walk down the same path he has chosen. He quickly got up and left only after a quick "fuck you", but not long after he came back and said! "No", I don't want my child to be like me – Then we had a decent conversation on how every one of these young men was also someone's child. He understood! I do know that I was not a very good role model to my own children. I remember often asking them; "do you want to grow up like me?" They always answered! "No!" That was very pleasing. Bottom-line! Only a fool shows others how to be a fool!

Title #47

Sister

Not trying to hurt you – or show you disgrace,

this point in your life – you need this slap to your face.

I never said I was perfect – something I didn't claim.

I am a fool sometimes – and I accept all the blame.

I'm pleased with my spirit – I'm pleased with my soul.

I will go to heaven – I will reach that goal.

Your heart has a problem – your evil inside.

You know the Lord's wants – but you do not abide.

From Darkness To The Wonderful Light

The demon of greed – you are caught in his mist.
The thing you hold dear – is cash in your fist.
Everything that you have – you've taken from men,
Be it one dollar bill – or be it a ten,
You lie to the government – to your man just the
same. But you point at all others – you should be
ashamed. Your wisdom, and knowledge – in these
points you're strong, But you're just like a bull – you
don't admit when you're wrong. When things do not
suit you – you bark you go mad, You're controlled by
the devil – it is pretty sad.
Never said I was righteous – you know that's no lie.
You need to take the pole – out of your eye.
The people you have – you have on a leash.
Just let it go – they'll be out of your reach.
Grandma died sinful – you know this is true.
You better wake up – or it will happen to you,
Again I'm not perfect – I repent every day,
I look at my faults – in every way.
I've done some things for you – never thrown in your
face. But for three packs of smokes – you gave me
disgrace.

From Darkness To The Wonderful Light

The paraphernalia you found – sure it was mine.

But I was gone for 8 months – or maybe gone nine.

If you stop using people – you'll stop feeling used,

I find it hard to believe – you feel so abused.

The pictures you have – the ones of yourself,

There thirty years old – take them off of the shelf.

You have the demon of hate – you hold it for Joe,

Please there, oh sister – please let it go.

In this lifetime of ours – I won't see you again.

There's a place that's called heaven – hope I see you

there then.

Statement of Enlightenment 47

Well this is a tough one. This poem was written directly to my sister. Though we had different Fathers and were in all actuality only half brother and sister. We never looked at it that way. I also have a younger sister that I really don't know too much about. I love them both dearly. The very few years that I did live under the same roof with my little sister. All I remember is that she was special, the baby, the white girl, and my step-father's true offspring. I also had an older sister who I grew up with only for short periods of time. My older sister had it very rough as a child also, the bad part is that for some reason it seemed as though her hardships were taken out on me quite often. Being the middle child was rough though. Daily I would get in trouble due to my little sister yelling out. "Mom, Dad, Peter hit me!" That lie always ended up in me getting grounded and getting hit upside the head with whatever was in arms reach. Then I had to deal with the daily ass beatings from my older sister. Believe it or not, I miss those days. I never got mad or can ever remember having an ill feeling against them. I knew that they genuinely loved me and I the same. This poem was written to my older sister. I do love her more than she knows. I remember as a child she would protect me and stick up for me in any situation. And then the next minute she was punching on me like "Gorilla gone wild" But that was OK, I accepted all issues from both of them like a grain of salt. We have had many great times together and could always look back and laugh at situations. I wrote this to her because the last time I saw her, she was battling a lot of demons. She is a fighter, and I just don't have it in my heart to partake in it. There is nothing I would not do for her. I stated that I felt she needed this slap to the face. But, do not take it wrong, it was written to solely slap her into reality and hopefully it will help her deal with the nightmare that she seems to live in. When I did spend time with her I gladly gave her my heart, arms, ears, back or the very little bit of money that I had. I accept her just as I except all. For whatever they are or however they are. As much as I love her, I just can't handle any more of the abuse. The physical abuse that ended when I grew was only taken over by mental abuse. And the way GOD has my heart working, does not allow me to fight with her. She can strike out a verbal blow like no other and I just don't want to strike back. I can handle getting my feelings hurt. What I can't deal with is hurting the feelings of someone that I love. Not saying that I don't or haven't, But I can honestly say "never on purpose or out of malice." I guess what I was trying to say that God loves all his children, the way they are now. Otherwise it would not be on record "Come as you are", to me that sounds like acceptance as we are in all are good or bad habits. When we can except that, then maybe we can except ourselves and others the same, and I also believe that no man or woman should try to take something that GOD has given each one of us. (Free Will). Who is more beautiful and powerful than God? That they should try to control another. Well I hope this sums it up. Even Jesus didn't make others walk as he did. And we all know of the last one that tried taking over GOD's job. Let "everything" go. Put life in GOD's hands, smile, enjoy life, and stop fighting life, love your Brother.

Title #48

Please

I've hurt myself plenty – and others the same.

Like a cloud that sheds darkness – I hold lots of

shame. I might stand on your heart – or beat your

flesh down. When the damage is past tense – I often

do frown. If by misfortune – Hates directed at you.

I hope you forgive me – I don't think I just do.

From Darkness To The Wonderful Light

I'm accustomed to destroying – my own life everyday.

So if you get hurt – please forgive me – you just got in

the way. I'll feel sorry for you – hell I feel sorry for me.

I don't want to be yours – or my own worst enemy,

I pray to God often – just about every day.

Where ever I'm at – or at night where I lay.

My pain it is real – you can't sense it or see.

But I want you to know – Its tormenting me.

I'm trying so hard – to cast my demons away,

I want the Lord in me – I want him to stay.

Statement of Enlightenment 48

Many may not gather from reading this, that I am a very sensitive person. Yeah! I know it sounds a little wispy washy, but it is true. It seemed that when growing up as a child, I was always on the bad end of physical and mental abuse. I can remember a great deal of times just wishing that I was somebody else, anyone except who I was. I was weak both physically and mentally. I had felt like a dog belly up most of the time. And I also remember doing a lot of crying. But that is something that I had kept to myself. I was very good at hiding my feelings. You see; while growing up I was told that crying was for girls, and if I showed the slightest inclination of sensitivity, that the response I knew I would get was; "toughen up, don't act like a girl" and it also seemed like daily, I was getting the shit beat out of me. Well! Growing up like this made me very good at hiding any weakness that I had, (I developed quite a poker face). Then everything changed, I toughened up. I was still very sensitive and still am. But I found out that sensitivity can bring results in two very different ways. Sorrow or rage. Being a little tired of the outcome of the sorrow, I turned it around to rage. But with GOD's help today, I have control over both.

Title #49

Institutionalized

I am in an institution for addicts, and the mentally
impaired. We are all in the system – We all need
special care.
I feel sorry for most – some are feeble and weak.
Others are addicts – throughout life its drugs that they
seek. For me I have issues of anger – despair.
I find the best place for me is here – under guidance
and care.

From Darkness To The Wonderful Light

I know that for some – there'll be no change their
whole life. They may not find loved ones – a husband
or wife Others are addicts – they have a two to one
chance. But it is hard to tell – cause they walk in a
trance. Others psychotic – they see and hear things not
real. I'm so glad, so blessed – that this isn't my deal.
I know I'm looking at others – the ones that I see.
My problems not obvious – it's the demons in me.
I have demons of anger – I have demons of rage.
I am glad I walked in here – and not drug to a cage.
I'm hoping medication – will pull me out of despair.
But most medication has me pulling out all my hair.
I'm praying for something different – when I walk out
of these doors. I don't want to go back – to violence,
drugs and the whores. I could have so much going – I
could have the world by the balls.
But I'm mostly in the gutters – self destruction its calls.
Its ok, I don't mind I can handle hurting me.
So I institutionalized myself – so I don't hurt the ones
that I see.

Statement of Enlightenment 49

This poem reflect on my life when I was a young man, maybe in my early twenties. Though I had already been involved with drugs for quite some time. That was not the main issue that I was dealing with. This was going on right when I got out of the Army and walked away from my suburb house and family. I think about it all the time. I had a wife that I still have some feelings for, and I also have a son that I have abandon. I was a very angry young man. Through my life as a child and up to that point of my life as a child and up to that point of my life in my twenties, I became very violent. I don't know why but I do know that I had the attitude that anyone who showed any anger, love, or looked at me as below them, would get hurt before I could give the chance to get hurt. I had beat down friends, robbed people, belittled, and overbeared all. As a child I was very ill, weak, and had a very low self-esteem. Uncles and Aunts told me that I was going to grow up in jail or dead at a young age. Several of the men in my Mother's life would torment me, to make it worse I grew up in the late 60"s, when if you were not White you were inferior, and wouldn't you know it. My Step-Fathers always moved us to small towns where I was the only minority that most have ever seen. And as we all know, children can be pretty cruel. Not to mention getting my ass beat daily by my own so called family. So when I reached puberty, something happened to my body and mind that gave me a great deal of power. I was faster and stronger than most that were twice my size. And also tough as hell. The mental and physical beatings that I had in the past, had created a monster. And I remember my Father living in a upper White middle class area when I went to stay with him for my first year of high school. Under one hundred pounds, on crutches, and the only minority. That's when I came to the point where I was no way in hell gonna take any more shit from people. The day the crutches went away was the day I started sending people to the doctors. I had a rage that was uncontrollable at times. Yes! That's right! I was a one hundred pound bully. The crazy spic that people avoided. And when I was in my 20's the rage heightened. I beat down my peers in the military, took the wives of other men, beat people and took from them. So this poem almost talking solely about myself. I held all these problems, and more. Today I am blessed, with God I'm not so destructive. I am at peace with myself and life.

Title #50

Useless to You

Have you even been beaten, forgotten, or left lying for
dead You may have done this to others, here's a
thought for your head
Have you signed off some family, because you thought
it was best
Did they burden your life; you felt you needed a rest
Say your parents or lover, no longer useful to you
Will you institutionalize or dump them, is that what to

do? I've befriended some elders that have been put in a home Family takes all their money, then their left to die all alone. They've given power of attorney, to the ones who've done this.

When he's dead and then buried, is the one that they'll miss Life can be hard; it could put a beating on a man's life. Dying alone, worse than a

Stab from a dull knife. These elders may not care, that they are dying, it's true. What may help their last days here, are just a visit or two. If you've done this to someone, I hope you have some regret. Because God knows of your heart, on this you can bet

Statement of Enlightenment 50

It's a sad thing when you think of all of the people that are looked at as worthless to society, more so than that is when sons, daughters, husbands and wives leave these that have been a big part in their life to die just like a dog in the pound they are getting robbed from their family members who have gotten power of attorney. I know of several men that have fought for this country and have stared death right in the face, solely so there family could live free in this life. Some that I have met have a monthly income of well over $7,000 a month, but are only giving $50.00 a week, because those that have power over their money feel that they don't need anything, the government is taking care of them, is their mentality, and worse than that is those that take all the benefits don't even bother to visit. I am one who holds a deep compassion in my heart. And it surely bothers me to know how many people, though may not be so called killers, they may as well be, as life, or this world will fight you to the last dying day, and a man is on his last breath, so many out there might as well be holding a pillow over the face of the almost dead. Ones parents or spouse may be in this situation, and not even remembered of the life that has been with them as a whole in the past. And those that have been hateful and mean who have been wished dead for most their lives, GOD will deal with them. If you could forgive people on their dying day or sooner, then that brings (You) closer to God, and then maybe you won't be judged as hateful when you're on your back dying. I can't, but if it were possible, it would be nice to be able to comfort all that have no-one, or all that are forgotten by everyone.

Title #51

There's Hope

I remember a time, I walked as a fool.
The devil he used me, just as his tool

Many saw a lost man; there was little hope
not in touch with the LORD, and also on dope

Some looked at me sideways, some they would laugh
they knew I was one, who would feel all GODS wrath

So many were righteous, that's in their own eye's
I surely was one that many despise

From Darkness To The Wonderful Light

I thank all the one's, that saw of my need
GOD worked in those people, they did plant a seed

I've come a long way, from the finger's that pointed
I was no lost cause, and today I'm anointed

Many looked at my flesh, never knew my inside
And today it's the lord, whom I solely confide

Now I am saved, I wish for others the same
To judge all my brother's, I won't hold that shame

I'll always remember, that I was the one
I was a man that many would shun

Remember GOD'S great, he's loving and kind
It's very important, to keep this in mind

No-one hopeless of saving, no matter the crime
GOD may touch all souls, but in his own time

Statement of Enlightenment 51

I was a visitor at a church when I was hit with the desire to write this poem. I had felt a little disgusted along with a little hurt when I heard this pastor judge a certain way that many of our youth present themselves. And when he as the pillar that he is enticed the congregation to judge and ridicule those youth that seem lost. Just as in the 60s when many thought GOD would send all those who grew their hair long, straight to hell, the facts are not any man who walks on this earth can know, (who's going where). And that no man is doomed! There is hope. Just as not so long ago, many saw me as doomed, and surely destined for Hell. The pastor was looking down at all are young gangster looking men. Just knowing that all those who wore their pants to low, were hopeless. Well, I believe that to be wrong, we never know who GOD will touch, or when. I feel that if your heart is truly with GOD, and you are walking Christ like to the best of your ability. If this is so, I think genuine concern and prayer are in need. GOD can save anyone; I remember reading that at one time David was considered hopeless. Many couldn't believe it when they found out that, he did a 180, then was one who was working for GOD. I feel that my life is somewhat similar. May be not to that extent, but never the less; once I spread darkness, and today I try to spread light, along with a little love. And as GOD has grabbed a hold of me, I want to hold on to others, not leave others in the rear. And one more thing, many gave up on me. But GOD didn't.

Title #52

Government Gangsters

This gang steals from thieves, and kills murderers to. These men are the finest, there the men dressed in blue.

This gang it's not just local, it's everywhere there nation- wide. There also in the phonebook, they have a badge they do not hide.

They may kick you; they may beat you, then carry you to a cell. A judge may ask; what happened? They say;

From Darkness To The Wonderful Light

"Your honor he fell.

The judge may not believe this, but they both work hand in hand. I suggest that you don't fight them; they'll pull you down just like quicksand.

If say a cop he has a bad day, and he hates himself and life. He may arrest you for no reason, then rape your precious wife.

If a man who has surrendered, hands behind him and he's quit. Some cops will ponce upon him, like flies upon some shit.

If you are the wrong color, or in the wrong neighborhood. Already you are guilty, as sure as trees are made of wood. Shaken baby syndrome, a thing a hateful nanny may do. Many law enforcement gangsters think the same way it is true.

I'm thankful for the videos, or many more men would be dead. Many cops don't pull the trigger, because of cameras overhead.

So if you are a saint, you hold GOD very dear many cops are like the devil, beware, some you should fear.

Statement of Enlightenment 52

I am not judging, I am merely stating a fact. And I am not referring to all officers of the law but merely a small percentage. Just as some Hispanics who are involved in the border wars involving drugs. They make all Hispanics look· bad. As the young black men that sling cocaine on the street corners make black men look bad. The Taliban and there vengeful strikes, make all Muslims look like killers. Well, the list could go on and on. What is true is that there is good and bad in all race's creeds, color, organizations, and in every individual the same. I'm sure you have heard the phrase "One bad apple don't spoil the whole bunch" true, but most won't see it that way. I do believe that there is a serious problem.I do understand that for their protection and the protection of others that force is sometimes a necessary. But come on! Sometimes it is sheer brutality. I believe that there should be a little more evaluations on who gets the honor and responsibility of being public servants. And don't get me wrong. Most officers are of good morals and values. Many have helped me and I do appreciate their service. I am merely disgusted with those that disrespect people but demand to have their asses kissed. A badge does not make them GOD's worthy of praise. Although, they do deserve and are worthy of respect, but some need to remember that respect is a two way street. Praise isn't so if you are reading this and it has hit a nerve. Maybe, just maybe it is written about you. And if you are one who doesn't feel this is a big deal. Try getting on your computer and checking out "Police Brutality" on you tube.

Title #53

Let Go

If you are a person, feeling hopeless with despair. I to knew these feelings, to them I am aware.

I once lived in darkness, my days had no light. No hope and self-pity, I had no insight.

I was truly excepting, and I was scared to make change. GOD seemed just like water, to a dog who has mange. I was told god could change me, that the now me it would die. But I am still me with GOD, what I heard was a lie.

From Darkness To The Wonderful Light

Facts are I was stupid, Satan had domination. In turn that made me, a complete abomination.

My heart changed dramatically, today I can feel. I am still who I was, only better for real.

GOD did not kill me, he just moved deep inside. So don't run from the lord, there's no reason to hide.

So just hold out your arms, and open your heart. Your life will be better, right from that start.

Not loving yourself, this feeling I know. Don't be afraid of GODS changes, please just let go.

Statement of Enlightenment 53

For many years of my life I felt lost and hopeless. Addiction, anger, and hate were a few of the problems and ill feelings that I held. On top of that my mindset was stuck on homicide and suicide most every day. When I looked in the mirror a sense of self-pity and shame spun around in my head. But on the other hand I held the false sense of power and strength. And I often wondered who or what could I be other than the man I saw in the mirror. My reflection did lie to me, it told me that I was a powerful force that could not be stopped and did not want to change. The fact was though, that I was to scared and weak to except the fact that I needed to change, I was living a lie. When I looked at others I saw weak and inferior people. But all those people had something that I didn't and I wanted it. All others seemed to be at peace and happy with who they were. And I was not familiar with that feeling. I knew only one thing, KAOS. And through all my years of kaos, god always popped up. Mostly in rehabs, jails, or mental wards. And so many people that had GOD in their lives would tell me, 'Pete just let go'. Then they would tell me that my life would change for the better, that I would be different. That the person that I was would die and I would be different. Well that scared the hell out of me. Who would I be? Would I get weak, turn into some kind of punk that I felt others to be? Well I did find GOD, I just had to open my eyes, heart and let go. And I found there was truth in some of what was being told to me. I changed in a very big way. I am a spirit! And one of GOD. And it happened almost overnight. And guess what, I am still the same person. But better than I thought was possible. Today I am at peace also excepting of who I am along with loving myself as I can love others. I really don't know how I could have been so blind to have gone through so many years without GOD in my life. And of course I still carry this flesh around, and I don't intend to lose it any time real soon. So that being said I am still just a man, a man that does feed the flesh. The big difference is that the devil no longer has dominion over it. I am not perfect by all means and I do have an occasional beer, get angry and have ill thoughts still. Again I am not perfect, only one was. And that would be JESUS, he is the only one I know of that walked a perfect walk. And every day I do grow. Today I am not fighting addiction, hate, or ill feelings toward others. And when I look in the mirror today I do not feel that my reflection is telling me a lie. It tells me that I did not lose what I was but I have gained what I was not. I cannot believe that I was scared to let the LORD into my life. And I must say it feels good not too be looked at as if I were a monster, or to feel like one myself I am not going through life today in total darkness. I am not going through life today with a stone for a heart. And I am defiantly not going through life today without GOD in my life. If you are one who is to scared, does not have the guts to let the LORD in your life. I hope someday you can, before it's too late. WHAT ARE YOU AFRAID OF? CAN GOD MAKE ANYONES LIFE ANY WORSE? LET GO!

Afterword

Today life is good, I feel blessed for the life that I have lived. As far as the future holds, I am somewhat clueless. Whatever the lord puts in my path, I will except and do the best I can to handle it in a Christ like was. I am taking all of the joy, sorrows, anger, and past feelings and try to apply them all in a positive way. And for the reason that I am merely a man, I may stumble from time to time. Though it is not my intension to do so, I am only a man! I will continue to keep GOD in my heart. I do have my vises, but I say again I am a man. Malice, deceit and hate will never be able to live in me, for GOD has changed that. Compassion for all is a big part of my life today and it will be tomorrow the same. I will love and except that I will not always get it back, but that's OK. I will be true to myself and others the same.

Page Intentionally Left Blank

Order Form

Website Orders: www.amazon.com
Mail Orders: Make checks or money order payable and address to:

W. James Johnson, Ph.D.

5807 Old Boyce Road

Alexandria, LA 71303

Telephone: 318-449-1497

Please send the following book:

_____ From Darkness To The Wonderful Light

Price: **$12.95**

Quantity: _____

Total Cost: _____

Name: _____

Address: _____

City: _____ State: _____ Zip: _____

Telephone: _____

Email Address: _____

Louisiana Residents Only Add 5% Sales Tax: _____

Shipping & Handling (Add $3.00 for first book and $1.00 for each additional book:

Total Amount Due: $ _____

Page Intentionally Left Blank

Order Form

Website Orders: www.amazon.com

Mail Orders: Make checks or money order payable and address to:

W. James Johnson, Ph.D.
5807 Old Boyce Road
Alexandria, LA 71303
Telephone: 318-449-1497

Please send the following book:

_____ From Darkness To The Wonderful Light

Price: $**12.95**

Quantity: _____

Total Cost: _____

Name: _____

Address: _____

City:_____ State: _____ Zip: _____

Telephone: _____

Email Address: _____

Louisiana Residents Only Add 5% Sales Tax: _____

Shipping & Handling (Add $3.00 for first book and $1.00 for each additional book:

Total Amount Due: $ _____

Notes

Notes

Notes

Made in the USA
Charleston, SC
28 January 2014